KNITTING
Sweaters
FOR KIDS

KNITTING
Sweaters
FOR KIDS

Consultant Editor ANGELA KENNEDY
Photographer STEVIE HUGHES

HARMONY BOOKS
New York

Published by Harmony Books, a division of Crown Publishers, Inc., 225 Park Avenue South, New York, New York 10003

Published in Great Britain by The National Magazine Co. Ltd., Colquhoun House, 27–37 Broadwick Street, London W1V 1FR

Harmony and colophon are trademarks of Crown Publishers, Inc.

Manufactured in Spain

Library of Congress Cataloging-in-Publication Data

Knitting sweaters for kids.
1. Knitting—Patterns.   2. Children's clothing.
3. Sweaters.   I. Kennedy, Angela.
TT825.K65   1986   646.4′5406   86–315
ISBN 0-517-56275-8
10 9 8 7 6 5 4 3 2 1

First American Edition

Edited by: Laurine Croasdale
Book Design by: Roger Daniels

Design Consultant: Debbie Bliss
Designers: Debbie Bliss, Tina Clark, Judy Dodson, Gay Hawkins, Joy Mountford, Mary Norden, Louise Parsons, Debbie Riehl, Debbie Scott
Assistant stylist: Sharon Ashworth
Technical Advisor: Marilyn Wilson

The publishers would like to thank the following for their assistance:
Mrs K Murphy, Mrs B Webb, Lindsay Plant, Margaret Yetton, Barbara Clarkson, Milly Johnson, Nellie Riehl, Hilary Usher, Janet Simpson, Mrs Neville, Pearl Elsmore, Marilyn Hiles, Lily Walsh, Mrs L Smith, Mrs Tracy, Miss Brittain, Mrs Mathews, Mrs Badrick, Mrs Coles, Pat Brooker, Avril Crawford, Sandra Hipperson, Jenny Trott.

ACKNOWLEDGEMENTS

Clothes from:	Fenwick, Mothercare, Benetton 012, New Man, Klimagers, Liberty, Cacharel, Dickins & Jones, The Scotch House, Now
Shoes from:	Russell & Bromley, Bally, Ravel, Mothercare, Lilley & Skinner
Glasses from:	First Sight, For Eyes
Hats from:	The Hat Shop, Liberty
Watches from:	Harvey Nichols, Tiq
Props from:	Astrohome, Force 4, Habitat, Harvey Nichols, Lillywhites, Liberty, Practical Styling

CONTENTS

INTRODUCTION

In these days of a hand knitting boom, it's hard to imagine why no-one has come up with the obvious, a book that's committed to hand knitting for children.

With the wealth of hand knitting books on sale children are the much missed out minority. They are usually wedged in between the pages of family knitting books or left to wallow amongst the clichéd cosy home-spun image of traditional ethnic knits.

This book is dedicated towards bringing a fresh attitude and energy towards knitting for children. No more dowdy ill-fitting sweaters, no more over laboured picture knits, here are easy roomy shapes for both boys and girls to enjoy wearing. Who can resist these brave bold colour blends that are striking and original? There are neon knits for bright sparks and mellow shades for whimsical tots. We make no fancy claims that these knits are art forms—in many cases they are just plain and simple styles that rely on a good quality fibre or clever colour to give them style and individuality. And as every knitter knows, the hardest pattern to find is often for the simplest of shapes.

There are quick to knit patterns for fast fashion results and fanciful Fair Isles that prove real labours of love—either way, welcome alternatives to shop bought styling. Whether you knit for pleasure, to create something individual or for sheer economy, *Knitting Sweaters for Kids* will appeal to all knitters and most importantly to all children the world over.

Angela Kennedy

BASIC INFORMATION

The flow of yarn which is controlled by the knitter is known as tension stitch gauge, and is as personal as handwriting. Some knitters put more stress on the yarn, making a smaller stitch and tighter knitted fabric; others put less stress on the yarn and make a looser fabric. For this reason a tension sample is essential for the success of your finished garment.

Why tension or stitch gauge is important
You must always measure the tension/stitch gauge before you start to make anything. This is necessary for two reasons: to check your tension/stitch gauge against the measurements given in a pattern, and to calculate the number of stitches to cast on and rows to work when you are planning a design of your own. The tension or stitch gauge is always given at the beginning of a pattern and states the number of stitches and rows to the centimetre or inch using the yarn, needles and stitch pattern for a given design.

Calculating the number of stitches and rows is known as tension or stitch gauging. Three factors influence this:
1 The size of needles and type of yarn.
2 The type of stitch pattern.
3 The knitter.

Making a tension/stitch gauge sample
Use the same yarn, needles and stitch pattern as those to be used for the main work. Knit a sample at least 12·5 × 12·5 cm/5 × 5 ins square. Smooth out the finished sample on a flat surface but do not stretch it.

Measuring the number of stitches
This determines the width of the knitting. Place a steel ruler or tape measure across the sample and mark 10 cm/4 ins across with pins. Count the number of stitches between the pins. For complete accuracy, pin out the sample several times. An extra half stitch will prove to be vital when you are working from a knitting pattern or when you are gauging the number of stitches to cast on for your own design.

Adjusting tension/stitch gauge
The tension/stitch gauge can be adjusted by changing the size of needles and working another sample. If there are too many stitches to the

centimetre or to the inch, your tension/stitch gauge is too tight and you should change to needles a size larger. If there are too few stitches, your tension/stitch gauge is too loose and you should change to needles a size smaller. If the number of stitches is correct but the number of rows incorrect, check the length as you proceed with the pattern.

Measuring the number of rows
This determines the depth of the knitting. The tension/stitch gauge also determines the number of rows to the centimetre or to the inch. Place a ruler vertically along the fabric and mark out 10 cm/4 ins with pins. Count the number of rows between the pins. From this count you can gauge the number of rows needed to reach the planned length of a design. You can also calculate where shaping is required and the position of increases and decreases.

UK/USA terminology
In the United Kingdom and the USA most knitting terms are the same. *Where they are different the UK term is given first.* For example terminology such as cast/bind off and the size of knitting needles (see chart below).

Altering a pattern
Always make a tension/stitch gauge sample if you intend to alter a pattern for example, changing from stocking/stockinette stitch to a lace stitch, or adding a cable panel. Also check the tension/stitch gauge when changing from a single colour to a multicolour pattern.

Garment care
A knitted garment will have a much longer life and better appearance if it is properly cared for. Always look on the ball band and check instructions for cleaning and pressing. Where the garment should be handwashed, wash in lukewarm water using a soap especially designed for knitwear. Do not leave to soak. Immerse garment and squeeze it gently, avoiding wringing or rubbing. Rinse thoroughly in tepid water, then gently squeeze to remove all excess water. Hold the garment at all times otherwise the weight will pull it out of shape. Place a towel on a table and dry the garment flat, patting it into shape. Dry away from direct heat.

Knitting Needle Sizes

English	000	00	0	1	2	3	4	5	6	7	8	9	10	11	12	13	14
Metric	10	9	8	7½	7	6½	6	5½	5	4½	4	3¾	3¼	3	2¾	2¼	2
American	15	13	12	11	10½	10	9	8	7	6	5	4	3	2	1	1	00

8

TWEEDY
TEAMSTERS

see page 46

TWEEDY
TEAMSTERS

see page 46

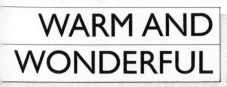

WARM AND WONDERFUL

see page 46

DOG AND DUCK

see page 48

CLASSIC POLO

see page 49

LOOSE CONNECTIONS

see page 50

ENGLISH
ROSE

see page 51

MOVIETIME MONO

see page 52

see page 53

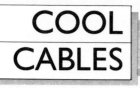

COOL CABLES

see page 54

SLICK KNITS

see page 55

BRIGHT SPARK

see page 57

STRIKER

see page 58

FAIR ISLE
RAMBLER

see page 59

HIKER'S HANDKNIT

see page 60

MELLOW
MELODY

see page 62

JAZZY JUMPER

see page 63

TYROLEAN TOUCH

see page 64

OLLY HOCKEY
STICKS

see page 65

WINSOME WAISTCOAT

see page 66

CASTAWAY

see page 67

IN THE SWING

see page 68

ALPHA
BETA

see page 69

see page 71

BOWLED
OVER

see page 72

DEMURE
AND DOTTY

see page 73

PUNCHY PRIMARIES

see page 74

DIAMOND DANDY

see page 75

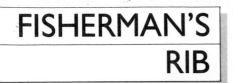

FISHERMAN'S RIB

see page 76

DEERSTALKER

see page 76

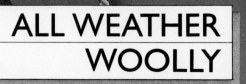

ALL WEATHER WOOLLY

see page 77

LACY
BOAT NECK

see page 78

SOLO
SWEATER

see page 79

see pages 8, 10

TWEEDY TEAMSTERS

Sizes

Chest	61(66:71:76) cm	24(26:28:30) in
Length	38(40:42:44) cm	15(15¾:16½:17¼) in
Sleeve Seam	26(28:30:32) cm	10¼(11:12:12½) in

Materials
3(3:4:4) 50 g/2 oz balls each of *Hayfield Grampian DK* in colours A and B.
One pair each 5½ mm/No. 9 and 6½ mm/No. 10½ knitting needles.
5½ mm/No. 9 circular needle.

Tension/gauge 15½ sts and 21 rows to 10 cm/4 in over st st on 6½ mm/No. 10½ needles.

Abbreviations Alt-alternate; beg-beginning; cm-centimetre(s); cont-continu(e)(ing); dec-decreas(e)(ing); foll-follow(s)(ing); g-gramme(s); in-inch(es); inc-increas(e)(ing); K-knit; mm-millimetre(s); No.-number; oz-ounce(s); P-purl; rem-remain(s)(ing); rep-repeat(ing); st(s)-stitch(es); st st-stocking stitch/stockinette stitch; sl-slip.

Note Use A and B together throughout.

BACK
** Using 5½ mm/No. 9 needles, cast on 48(52:56:60) sts.
Cont in K1, P1 rib until work measures 5 cm/2 in from beg, ending with a right side row.
Next row Rib 6(7:5:7), * inc in next st, rib 3(3:4:4), rep from * to last 6(9:6:8) sts, inc in next st, rib to end. 58(62:66:70) sts. **
Change to 6½ mm/No. 10½ needles. Beg with a K row, cont in st st until work measures 38(40:42:44) cm/ 15(15¾:16½:17¼) in from beg, ending with a P row.
Shape Shoulders
Cast/bind off 9(9:10:10) sts at beg of next 2 rows and 9(10:10:11) sts at beg of foll 2 rows. Leave rem 22(24:26:28) sts on a spare needle.

FRONT
Work as for Back from ** to **.
Change to 6½ mm/No. 10½ needles. Beg with a K row, cont in st st until work measures 31(33:34:36) cm/ 12¼(13:13½:14¼) in from beg, ending with a P row.

Shape Neck
Next row K22(23:24:25) sts and turn leaving rem sts on a spare needle, P to end.
Cont on these sts only for left side of neck.
Dec one st at neck edge on next and every foll alt row until 18(19:20:21) sts rem.
Cont without shaping until work matches Back to shoulder, ending at armhole edge.
Shape Shoulder
Cast/bind off 9(9:10:10) sts at beg of next row.
Work 1 row. Cast/bind off rem 9(10:10:11) sts.
With right side of work facing, return to sts on spare needle. Sl centre 14(16:18:20) sts onto a stitch holder, rejoin yarns at inner edge, K to end.
Complete to match first side of neck.

SLEEVES
Using 5½ mm/No. 9 needles, cast on 26(28:30:32) sts.
Cont in K1, P1 rib until work measures 5 cm/2 in from beg, ending with a right side row.
Next row Rib 5(6:6:7), * inc in next st, rib 4(4:5:5), rep from * to last 6(7:6:7) sts, inc in next st, rib to end. 30(32:34:36) sts.
Change to 6½ mm/No. 10½ needles. Beg with a K row cont in st st inc one st at each end of next and every foll 3rd(4th:4th:4th) row until there are 54(56:58:60) sts.
Cont without shaping until work measures 26(28:30:32) cm/10¼(11:12:12½) in from beg, ending with a P row.
Cast/bind off **loosely**.

TO MAKE UP
Join shoulder seams.

POLO COLLAR
With right side of work facing, using 5½ mm/No. 9 circular needle, K up 12 sts down left side of neck, K14(16:18:20) sts from front neck, K up 12 sts up right side of neck and K across 22(24:26:28) sts on back neck. 60(64:68:72) sts.
Work in rounds of K1, P1 rib until collar measures 10 cm/ 4 in from beg.
Cast/bind off **loosely** in rib.
Set in sleeves, placing centre of cast/bound off edge to shoulder seam. Join side and sleeve seams.

---

see page 11

WARM AND WONDERFUL

Sizes

Chest	61(66:71:77) cm	24(26:28:30) in
Length	51(56:61:66) cm	20(22:24:26) in
Sleeve Seam	27(31:36:39) cm	10½(12¼:14:15½) in

Materials
12(13:14:15) 50 g/2 oz balls of *Sirdar Country Style Chunky*.
One pair each 5 mm/No. 8 and 6 mm/No. 10 knitting needles.
5 mm/No. 8 circular needle.
Cable needle.

Tension/gauge 15 sts and 20 rows to 10 cm/4 in over moss st patt on 6 mm/No. 10 needles.

Abbreviations Alt-alternate; beg-beginning; cm-centimetre(s); cont-continu(e)(ing); dec-decreas(e)(ing); foll-follow(s)(ing); g-gramme(s); in-inch(es); inc-increas(e)(ing); inc R-increase right, K into the back of the st in the row below next st on left hand needle, then K st on needle; inc L-increase left, K into the front of the st in the row below next st on left hand needle, then K st on needle; K-knit; mm-millimetre(s); MB-make bobble-[K1, P1, K1, P1, K1] all into next st, lift 1st, 2nd, 3rd and 4th sts over 5th st and off needle; No.-number; oz-ounce(s); P-purl; patt-pattern; p2sso-pass 2 slipped sts over; rep-repeat(ing); rem-remain(s)(ing); st(s)-stitch(es); sl-slip; T2R-twist 2 right, K2 tog, but do not drop sts off needle, K first st again, allow sts to drop off needle; T2L-twist 2 left, K tbl 2nd st on left hand needle, then K first and 2nd sts tog tbl; tbl-through back of loop(s); tog-together.

PATT PANEL A (worked over 13 sts)
1st row (wrong side) K3, P1, K1, P2, K2, P1, K3.
2nd row P3, T2L, P1, T2L, T2R, P3.
3rd row K4, P2, K2, P1, K4.
4th row P2, MB, P1, T2L, P1, T2R, P4.
5th row K4, P2, K1, P1, K2, P1, K2.
6th row P2, T2L, P1, K1 tbl, T2R, T2L, P3.
7th row K3, P1, K2, P2, K1, P1, K3.
8th row P3, T2L, T2R, P1, T2R, P3.
9th row K4, P1, K2, P2, K4.
10th row P4, T2L, P1, T2R, P1, MB, P2.
11th row K2, P1, K2, P1, K1, P2, K4.
12th row P3, T2R, T2L, K1 tbl, P1, T2R, P2.
These 12 rows form patt panel A.

PATT PANEL B (worked over 19 sts)
1st row (wrong side) K6, [P1, K1] 3 times, P1, K6.
2nd row P5, T2R, [K1, P1] twice, K1, T2L, P5.
3rd row K5, P2, [K1, P1] 3 times, P1, K5.
4th row P4, T2R, [P1, K1] 3 times, P1, T2L, P4.
5th row K4, [P1, K1] 5 times, P1, K4.
6th row P3, T2R, [K1, P1] twice, (K1, P1, K1) all into next st, [P1, K1] twice, T2L, P3.
7th row K3, P2, K1, P1, K1, P5, K1, P1, K1, P2, K3.
8th row P2, T2R, [P1, K1] twice, P1, inc R, K1, inc L, P1, [K1, P1] twice, T2L, P2.
9th row K2, [P1, K1] 3 times, P7, [K1, P1] 3 times, K2.
10th row P2, K1 tbl, [K1, P1] 3 times, inc R, K3, inc L, [P1, K1] 3 times, K1 tbl, P2.
11th row K2, [P1, K1] 3 times, P9, [K1, P1] 3 times, K2.
12th row P2, K1 tbl, [K1, P1] 3 times, K2, sl 2, K1, p2sso, K2, [P1, K1] 3 times, K1 tbl, P2.
13th row As 9th row.
14th row P2, K1 tbl, [K1, P1] 3 times, K1, sl 2, K1, p2sso, K1, [P1, K1] 3 times, K1 tbl, P2.
15th row K2, [P1, K1] 3 times, P5, [K1, P1] 3 times, K2.
16th row P2, K1 tbl, [K1, P1] 3 times, sl 2, K1, p2sso, [P1, K1] 3 times, K1 tbl, P2.
17th row K2, [P1, K1] 3 times, P3, [K1, P1] 3 times, K2.
18th row P2, T2L, P1, K1, P1, T2R, K1, T2L, P1, K1, P1, T2R, P2.
19th row K3, P2, K1, [P3, K1] twice, P2, K3.
20th row P3, T2L, K1, T2R, P1, K1, P1, T2L, K1, T2R, P3.
These 20 rows form patt panel B.

BACK
** Using 5 mm/No. 8 needles, cast on 56(64:72:80) sts.
Cont in K1, P1 rib until work measures 8(8:10:10) cm/ 3(3:4:4) in from beg, ending with a wrong side row.
Next row Rib 7(4:8:5), * inc in next st, rib 2(3:3:4), rep from * to last 7(4:8:5) sts, inc in next st, rib to end. 71(79:87:95) sts.
Change to 6 mm/No. 10 needles and cont in patt as foll:
1st row (wrong side) [K2, P2] 3(4:5:6) times, work 1st row patt panel A, P1, work 1st row patt panel B, P1, work 1st row patt panel A, [K2, P2] 3(4:5:6) times.
2nd row [K2, P2] 3(4:5:6) times, work 2nd row patt panel A, K1, work 2nd row patt panel B, K1, work 2nd row patt panel A, [K2, P2] 3(4:5:6) times.
3rd row [P2, K2] 3(4:5:6) times, work 3rd row patt panel A, P1, work 3rd row patt panel B, P1, work 3rd row patt panel A, [P2, K2] 3(4:5:6) times.
4th row [P2, K2] 3(4:5:6) times, work 4th row patt panel A, K1, work 4th row patt panel B, K1, work 4th row patt panel A, [P2, K2] 3(4:5:6) times.
These 4 rows establish the patt, placing patt panels and edge sts in moss st patt.
Keeping patt correct cont until work measures 34(36:39:41) cm/13½(14:15½:16¼) in from beg, ending with a wrong side row.
Shape Armholes
Cast/bind off 6 sts at beg of next 2 rows. 59(67:75:83) sts. **
Cont without shaping until work measures 51(56:61:66) cm/20(22:24:26) in from beg, ending with a wrong side row.
Shape Shoulders
Cast/bind off 20(23:25:27) sts at beg of next 2 rows.
Leave rem 19(21:25:29) sts on a spare needle.

FRONT
Work as given for Back from ** to **.
Cont without shaping until work measures 44(48:53:57) cm/17½(19:21:22½) in from beg, ending with a wrong side row.
Shape Neck
Next row Patt 24(27:31:35) sts, cast/bind off next 11(13:13:13) sts, patt to end.
Complete right side of neck first.
Next row Patt to end.
Next row Cast/bind off 2 sts, patt to end.
Rep last 2 rows until 20(23:25:27) sts rem.
Cont without shaping until work measures same as Back to shoulder, ending at armhole edge.
Shape Shoulder
Cast/bind off rem sts.
With wrong side of work facing return to sts for left side of neck, rejoin yarn at neck edge patt to end.
Complete to match first side of neck.

SLEEVES
Using 5 mm/No. 8 needles, cast on 27(29:31:33) sts.
Cont in K1, P1 rib as foll:
1st row (right side) K1, * P1, K1, rep from * to end.
2nd row P1, * K1, P1, rep from * to end.
Rep these 2 rows until work measures 8 cm/3 in from beg, ending with a wrong side row.
Next row Rib 6(7:8:9), * inc in next st, rep from * to last 7(8:9:10) sts, rib to end. 41(43:45:47) sts.
Change to 6 mm/No. 10 needles and cont in patt as foll:
1st row Moss st patt 11(12:13:14), work 1st row patt panel B, moss st patt to end.
This row establishes the patt, placing patt panel and edge sts in moss st patt as given for Back. Cont, keeping patt correct, inc one st at each end of every foll 4th row until there are 53(61:69:77) sts.
Cont without shaping until work measures 31(35:40:43) cm/12¼(13¾:16:17) in from beg, ending with a wrong side row. Cast/bind off **loosely**.

TO MAKE UP
Join shoulder seams.

COLLAR
With right side of work facing, using 5 mm/No. 8 circular needle, beg at centre front neck, K up 5(6:6:6) sts at centre front, K up 11(13:15:17) sts up right front neck, K across 19(21:25:27) sts at back neck, K up 11(13:15:17) sts down left side of neck, then 6(7:7:7) from centre front neck. 52(60:68:74) sts.
Work in rounds of K1, P1 rib. Work 4 rounds, ending at centre front.
Next round Rib 22(26:30:34), [work 3 times into next st, rib 1] 3 times, work 3 times into next st, rib to end. 60(68:76:82) sts.
Now cont to work in rows, backwards and forwards.
Cont in rib until collar measures 9(9:11:11) cm/ 3½(3½:4½:4½) in from beg. Cast/bind off in rib.
Set in sleeves, joining final rows to cast/bound off sts at underarm. Join side and sleeve seams.

see page 12

DOG AND DUCK

Sizes

Chest	61(66:71:76) cm	24(26:28:30) in
Length	38(40:42:44) cm	15(16:16½:17½) in
Sleeve Seam	27(31:35:39) cm	10½(12¼:13¾:15½) in

Materials
5(5:6:6) 50 g/2 oz balls of *Schachenmayer Nomotta Extra* in main colour A.
2(2:2:2) balls in contrast colour B.
Oddment for embroidery.
One pair each 3 mm/No. 3 and 3¾ mm/No. 5 knitting needles.

Tension/gauge 24 sts and 32 rows to 10 cm/4 in over st st on 3¾ mm/No. 5 needles.

Abbreviations Beg-beginning; cm-centimetre(s); cont-continue(e)(ing); dec-decreas(e)(ing); foll-follow(s)(ing); g-gramme(s); in-inch(es); inc-increas(e)(ing); K-knit; mm-millimetre(s); M1-make one, pick up the bar that lies between st just worked and next st and work into the back of it; No.-number; oz-ounce(s); P-purl; patt-pattern; rem-remain(s)(ing); rep-repeat(ing); st(s)-stitch(es); st st-stocking stitch/stockinette stitch; sl-slip.

BACK
** Using 3 mm/No. 3 needles and A, cast on 72(78:84:90) sts. Cont in K1, P1 rib until work measures 7(7:8:8) cm/2¾(2¾:3:3) in from beg, ending with a right side row.
Next row Rib 6(9:2:5) * M1, rib 3(3:4:4), rep from * to last 6(9:2:5) sts, M1, rib to end. 93(99:105:111) sts.
Change to 3¾ mm/No. 5 needles and cont in st st, beg with a K row working from chart. Read K rows from right to left and P rows from left to right. **
Cont until work measures 38(40:42:44) cm/15(16:16½:17½) in from beg, ending with a P row.
Shape Shoulders
Cast/bind off 16(17:18:19) sts at beg of next 4 rows.
Leave rem 29(31:33:35) sts on a spare needle.

FRONT
Work as given for Back from ** to **.
Cont until work measures 33(34:36:38) cm/13(13½:14¼:15) in from beg, ending with a P row.
Shape Neck

Next row Patt 40(42:44:46) sts and turn, leaving rem sts on a spare needle.
Complete left side of neck first.
Dec one st at neck edge on every row until 32(34:36:38) sts rem.
Cont without shaping until work measures same as Back to shoulder, ending at armhole edge.
Shape Shoulder
Cast/bind off 16(17:18:19) sts at beg of next row.
Work 1 row. Cast/bind off rem 16(17:18:19) sts.
With right side of work facing, return to sts on spare needle. Sl centre 13(15:17:19) sts onto a stitch holder, rejoin yarn at neck edge, patt to end.
Complete to match left side of neck.

SLEEVES
Using 3 mm/No. 3 needles and A, cast on 34(36:38:40) sts. Cont in K1, P1 rib until work measures 4(4:5:5) cm/1½(1½:2:2) in from beg, ending with a right side row.
Next row Rib 1(2:1:2), * M1, rib 2, rep from * to last 1(2:1:2) sts, M1, rib to end. 51(53:57:59) sts.
Change to 3¾ mm/No. 5 needles and beg with a K row cont in st st working from chart, **at the same time**, inc and work into patt, one st at each end of 3rd and every foll 5th row until there are 75(81:85:89) sts.
Cont without shaping until work measures 27(31:35:39) cm/10½(12¼:13¾:15½) in from beg, ending with a P row.
Cast/bind off **loosely**.

TO MAKE UP
Join right shoulder seam.

NECKBAND
With right side of work facing, using 3 mm/No. 3 needles and A, K up 23(24:25:26) sts down left side of neck, K across 13(15:17:19) sts at centre front, inc 2 sts, K up 23(24:25:26) sts up right side of neck, K across 29(31:33:35) sts at back neck, inc 5 sts evenly. 95(101:107:113) sts.
Next row P1, * K1, P1, rep from * to end.
Next row K1, * P1, K1, rep from * to end.
Rep the last 2 rows until neckband measures 7(7:8:8) cm/2¾(2¾:3:3) in from beg. Cast/bind off **loosely** in rib.
Join left shoulder and neckband seam.
Fold neckband in half onto wrong side and catch down.
Set in sleeves, placing centre of cast/bound off edge to shoulder seam. Join side and sleeve seams. Embroider eyes and collars and add bows.

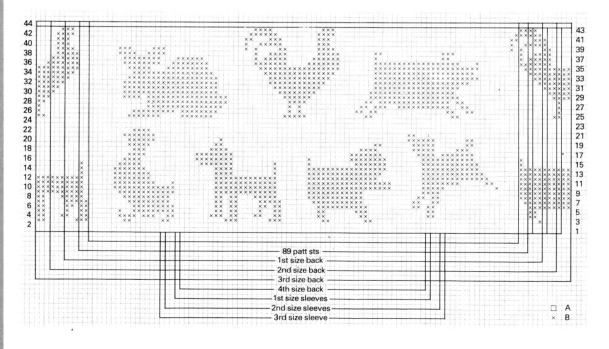

see page 13

CLASSIC POLO

Sizes

Chest	61(66:71:76) cm	24(26:28:30) in
Length	41(45:49:56) cm	16¼(17¾:19¼:22) in
Sleeve Seam	29(33:37:41) cm	11½(13:14½:16¼) in

Materials

9(10:11:13) 50 g/2 oz balls of *Scheepjeswol Superwash Zermatt*.

One pair each 3¼ mm/No. 4, 4 mm/No. 6 and 4½ mm/ No. 7 knitting needles.

Cable needle.

Tension/gauge 21 sts and 28 rows to 10 cm/4 in over rev st st on 4½ mm/No. 7 needles.

Abbreviations Alt-alternate; beg-beginning; cm-centimetre(s); cont-continu(e)(ing); C4B-sl next 2 sts onto cable needle and hold at back of work, K2 then K2 from cable needle; C4F-sl next 2 sts onto cable needle and hold at front of work, K2 then K2 from cable needle; Cr3B-sl next st onto cable needle and hold at back of work, K2, then K1 from cable needle; Cr3F-sl next 2 sts onto cable needle and hold at front of work, K1 then K2 from cable needle; dec-decreas(e)(ing); foll-follow(s)(ing); g-gramme(s); in-inch(es); inc-increas(e)(ing); K-knit; mm-millimetre(s); M1-make one, pick up the bar that lies between st just worked and next st and work into back of it; No.-number; oz-ounce(s); P-purl; patt-pattern; rem-remain(s)(ing); rep-repeat(ing); rev st st-reverse stocking stitch/ stockinette stitch; st(s)-stitch(es); sl-slip; tog-together.

PATT PANEL A (worked over 12 sts)

1st row (right side) K2, P2, K4, P2, K2.
2nd row P2, K2, P4, K2, P2.
3rd–6th rows Rep 1st–2nd rows twice.
7th row Sl next 4 sts onto cable needle and hold at back of work, K2 then P2, K2 from cable needle, sl next 2 sts onto cable needle and hold at front of work, K2, P2, then K2 from cable needle.
8th row As 2nd row.
9th–13th rows Rep 1st–2nd rows twice, then work 1st row again.
14th row K.
15th–16th rows Rep 14th row twice.
These 16 rows form patt panel A.

PATT PANEL B (worked over 10 sts)

1st row (right side) P3, C4B, P3.
2nd and every foll alt row K the P sts and P the K sts of previous row.
3rd row P2, Cr3B, Cr3F, P2.
5th row P1, Cr3B, K2, Cr3F, P1.
7th row Cr3B, K4, Cr3F.
8th row As 2nd row.
These 8 rows form patt panel B.

PATT PANEL C (worked over 10 sts)

1st row (right side) P3, C4F, P3.
2nd and every foll alt row K the P sts and P the K sts of previous row.
3rd–8th rows Rep 3rd–8th rows of patt panel B.
These 8 rows form patt panel C.

BACK

** Using 3¼ mm/No. 4 needles, cast on 69(75:79:87) sts.
Cont in K1, P1 rib as foll:
1st row (right side) K1, * P1, K1, rep from * to end.
2nd row P1, * K1, P1, rep from * to end.
Rep these 2 rows until work measures 5 cm/2 in from beg, ending with a right side row.
Next row Rib 5(3:5:4), M1, * rib 6(7:7:8), M1, rep from * to last 4(2:4:3) sts, rib to end. 80(86:90:98) sts.
Change to 4½ mm/No. 7 needles and cont in patt as foll:
1st row (right side) [K1, P1] 1(2:2:4) times, K1,
P3(3:4:4), work 1st row patt panel A, P3(3:4:4), work 1st row patt panel B, P3(4:4:4), work 1st row patt panel A, P3(4:4:4), work 1st row patt panel C, P3(3:4:4), work 1st row patt panel A, P3(3:4:4), K1, [P1, K1] 1(2:2:4) times.
2nd row [P1, K1] 1(2:2:4) times, P1, K3(3:4:4), work 2nd row patt panel A, K3(3:4:4), work 2nd row patt panel C, K3(4:4:4), work 2nd row patt panel A, K3(4:4:4), work 2nd row patt panel B, K3(3:4:4), work 2nd row patt panel A, K3(3:4:4), P1, [K1, P1] 1(2:2:4) times.
3rd row [P1, K1] 1(2:2:4) times, P4(4:5:5), work 3rd row patt panel A, P3(3:4:4), work 3rd row patt panel B, P3(4:4:4), work 3rd row patt panel A, P3(4:4:4), work 3rd row patt panel C, P3(3:4:4), work 3rd row patt panel A, P4(4:5:5), [K1, P1] 1(2:2:4) times.
4th row [K1, P1] 1(2:2:4) times, K4(4:5:5), work 4th row patt panel A, K3(3:4:4), work 4th row patt panel C, K3(4:4:4), work 4th row patt panel A, K3(4:4:4), work 4th row patt panel B, K3(3:4:4), work 4th row patt panel A, K4(4:5:5), [P1, K1] 1(2:2:4) times.
These 4 rows establish the patt, placing the patt panels and edge sts in double moss st patt.
Keeping patt panels correct, cont until work measures 26(29:32:37) cm/10(11½:12½:14½) in from beg, ending with a wrong side row.

Shape Armholes

Cast/bind off 3(4:5:6) sts at beg of next 2 rows. 74(78:80:86) sts. **
Cont without shaping until work measures 15(16:17:19) cm/6(6¼:6½:7½) in from beg of armhole shaping, ending with a wrong side row.

Shape Shoulders and Back Neck

Next row Patt 27(28:29:30) sts and turn, leaving rem sts on a spare needle.
Complete right side of back neck first.
Next row Patt 4 sts and sl onto a safety pin, patt to end.
Next row Cast/bind off 11(12:12:13), patt to last 2 sts, work 2 tog.
Work 1 row.
Cast/bind off rem 11(11:12:12) sts.
With right side of work facing, return to sts on spare needle. Sl centre 20(22:22:26) sts onto a stitch holder, rejoin yarn at neck edge patt to end.
Next row Patt to end.
Complete to match first side of neck.

FRONT

Work as given for Back from ** to **.
Keeping patt panels correct, cont until work measures 12(12:14:14) rows less than Back to shoulder, ending with a wrong side row.

Shape Neck

Next row Patt 30(31:32:33) sts, work 2 tog and turn, leaving rem sts on a spare needle.
Complete left side of neck first.
Dec one st at neck edge on foll 8(8:6:6) rows, then at same edge on every foll alt row until 22(23:24:25) sts rem, ending at armhole edge.

Shape Shoulder

Cast/bind off 11(12:12:13) sts at beg of next row.
Work 1 row. Cast/bind off rem 11(11:12:12) sts.
With right side of work facing, return to sts on spare needle. Sl centre 10(12:12:16) sts onto a stitch holder, rejoin yarn at neck edge, work 2 tog, patt to end. 31(32:33:34) sts.
Complete to match first side of neck.

SLEEVES

Using 3¼ mm/No. 4 needles, cast on 34(36:40:42) sts.
Cont in K1, P1 rib until work measures 4 cm/1½ in from beg, ending with a right side row.
Next row Rib 3(2:3:2), M1, * rib 1, M1, rib 2, M1, rep from * to last 4 sts, rib 2, M1, rib 2. 54(58:64:68) sts.
Change to 4½ mm/No. 7 needles and cont in patt as foll:

1st and 2nd Sizes Only

1st row (right side) P0(1), [K1, P1] 3 times, P2, work 1st row patt panel B, P3(4), work 1st row patt panel A,

P3(4), work 1st row patt panel C, P2, [P1, K1] 3 times, P0(1).

2nd row K0(1), [P1, K1] 3 times, K2, work 2nd row patt panel C, K3(4), work 2nd row patt panel A, K3(4), work 2nd row patt panel B, K2, [K1, P1] 3 times, K0(1).

These 2 rows establish the patt, placing patt panels and edge sts in double moss st patt. Keeping panels correct, cont inc and working into moss st, one st at each end of 5th and every foll 8th row until there are 70(76) sts.

3rd and 4th Sizes Only

1st row P1(3), C4B, P7, work 1st row patt panel B, P4, work 1st row patt panel A, P4, work 1st row patt panel C, P7, C4F, P1(3).

2nd row K1(3), P4, K7, work 2nd row patt panel C, K4, work 2nd row patt panel A, K4, work 2nd row patt panel B, K7, P4, K1(3).

These 2 rows establish the patt, placing patt panels with patt panels B and C at edge sts. Keeping panels correct, cont inc one st at each end of 5th and every foll 8th row until there are 82(92) sts, then every foll 6th row until there are 86(94) sts, working extra sts to complete patt panels B and C, working 4 sts rev st st, then into double moss st patt.

All Sizes

Cont without shaping until work measures 30(35:40:44) cm/12(13¾:16:17½) in from beg, ending with a wrong side row.

Cast/bind off **loosely**.

TO MAKE UP

Join right shoulder seam.

POLO COLLAR

With right side of work facing, using 3¼ mm/No. 4 needles, K up 16(17:19:19) sts down left side of neck, K across 10(12:12:16) sts at centre front, K up 16(17:19:19) sts up right side of neck, 3 sts down right back neck, K across 28(30:30:34) sts at centre back neck, K up 3 sts up left back neck. 76(82:86:94) sts.

Cont in K1, P1 rib until collar measures 5(5:6:6) cm/ 2(2:2½:2½) in from beg.

Change to one 3¼ mm/No. 4 needle and one 4 mm/No. 6 needle. Rib 6 rows.

Change to 4 mm/No. 6 needles and cont in rib until collar measures 12(12:16:16) cm/4¾(4¾:6¼:6¼) in from beg. Cast/bind off **loosely** in rib.

Join left shoulder seam and polo collar, reversing seam for half of collar to turn back.

Set in sleeves, sewing final rows to sts cast/bound off at underarm.

Join side and sleeve seams.

see page 14

LOOSE CONNECTIONS

Sizes

Chest	61(66:71:76) cm	24(26:28:30) in
Length	45(50:53:58) cm	17¾(19¾:21:23) in
Sleeve Seam	27(32:37:38) cm	10¾(12½:14½:15) in

Materials

7(8:8:9) 25 g/1 oz balls of *Argyll Finesse Mohair* in main colour A.

One 50 g/2 oz ball of *Argyll Nice 'n' Easy Double Crepe* in each of 3 contrast colours B, C and D.

One pair each 3¼ mm/No. 4 and 5 mm/No. 8 knitting needles.

Tension/gauge 15 sts and 20 rows to 10 cm/4 in over st st using A on 5 mm/No. 6 needles.

Abbreviations Alt-alternate; beg-beginning; cm-centimetre(s); cont-continu(e)(ing); dec-decreas(e)(ing); foll-follow(s)(ing); g-gramme(s); in-inch(es); inc-increas(e)(ing); K-knit; mm-millimetre(s); No.-number; oz-ounce(s); P-purl; rem-remain(s)(ing); rep-repeat(ing); st(s)-stitch(es); st st-stocking stitch/stockinette stitch; sl-slip; tog-together.

BACK

** Using 3¼ mm/No. 4 needles and B, cast on 67(73:77:83) sts. Cont in K1, P1 rib as foll:

1st row K1, * P1, K1, rep from * to end.

2nd row P1, * K1, P1, rep from * to end.

Rep these 2 rows until work measures 5 cm/2 in from beg, ending with a 1st row.

Next row Rib 4(1:5:2), * work 2 tog, rib 2, work 2 tog, rib 3, rep from * to end. 53(57:61:65) sts. **

Change to 5 mm/No. 8 needles and A. Beg with a K row cont in st st until work measures 45(50:53:58) cm/ 17¾(19¾:21:23) in from beg, ending with a P row.

Shape Shoulders

Cast/bind off 18(19:21:22) sts at beg of next 2 rows.

Leave rem 17(19:19:21) sts on a spare needle.

FRONT

Work as for Back from ** to **.

Change to 5 mm/No. 8 needles and A. Beg with a K row cont in st st until work measures 39(44:47:52) cm/ 15½(17¼:18½:20½) in from beg, ending with a P row.

Shape Neck

Next row K21(22:24:25), K2 tog, turn leaving rem sts on a spare needle. Cont on these sts only for left side of neck.

Dec one st at neck edge on next 2 rows then on 2 foll alt rows. 18(19:21:22) sts.

Cont without shaping until work matches Back to shoulder, ending with a P row.

Shape Shoulder

Cast/bind off rem sts.

With right side of work facing, return to sts on spare needle. Sl centre 7(9:9:11) sts onto a safety pin, rejoin yarn at inner neck edge, K to end. Complete to match first side of neck, reversing all shapings.

SLEEVES

Using 3¼ mm/No. 4 needles and C, cast on 39(41:41:41) sts. Cont in K1, P1 rib as for Back until work measures 5 cm/2 in from beg, ending with a 1st row.

Next row Rib 6(7:4:4), inc in next st, * rib 12(12:7:7), inc in next st, rep from * to last 6(7:4:4) sts, rib to end. 42(44:46:46) sts.

Change to 5 mm/No. 8 needles and A. Beg with a K row cont in st st, inc one st at each end of 7th(7th:9th:9th) row and every foll 6th(8th:9th:8th) row until there are 54(56:58:60) sts.

Cont without shaping until work measures 27(32:37:38) cm/10¾(12½:14½:15) in from beg, ending with a P row. Cast/bind off **loosely**.

TO MAKE UP

Join right shoulder seam.

NECKBAND

Using 3¼ mm/No. 4 needles and D, and with right side of work facing, K up 15 sts down left side of neck, K across 7(9:9:11) sts at front, K up 15 sts up right side of neck and K across 17(19:19:21) sts at back neck. 54(58:58:62) sts.

Next row P1(3:3:1), [inc in next st, P1, inc in next st, P1] 4(4:4:5) times across back neck sts, P15, P1(2:0:1) inc in next st, [P1, inc in next st] 2(2:4:4) times, P1(2:0:1) across front sts, P15. 65(69:71:77) sts.

Cont in K1, P1 rib as for Back until neckband measures 6 cm/2½ in from beg.

Cast/bind off in rib using a 5 mm/No. 8 needle.

Join left shoulder and neckband. Fold neckband in half onto wrong side and catch down.

Set in sleeves, placing centre of cast/bound off edge to shoulder seams. Join side and sleeve seams.

see page 16

ENGLISH ROSE

Sizes

Chest	61(66:71:76) cm	24(26:28:30) in
Length	42(46:49:53) cm	16½(18:19¼:21) in
Sleeve Seam	27(31:36:39) cm	10½(12¼:14¼:15½) in

Materials

2(3:3:4) 50 g/2 oz balls of *Lister Motoravia* 4 ply in main colour A.
2(2:2:2) balls in contrast colour B.
1(1:1:1) ball in contrast colour C.
One pair each 2¾ mm/No. 2 and 3¼ mm/No. 4 knitting needles.

Tension/gauge 28 sts and 30 rows to 10 cm/4 in over st st on 3¼ mm/No. 4 needles.

> **Abbreviations** Approx-approximately; alt-alternate; beg-beginning; cm-centimetre(s); cont-continu(e)(ing); dec-decreas(e)(ing); foll-follow(s)(ing); in-inch(es); g-gramme(s); inc-increas(e)(ing); K-knit; mm-millimetre(s); M1-make one by picking up the bar that lies between st just worked and next st and working into the back of it; No.-number; oz-ounce(s); P-purl; patt-pattern; rem-remain(s)(ing); rep-repeat(ing); st(s)-stitch(es); sl-slip; tog-together.

BACK

** Using 2¾ mm/No. 2 needles and A, cast on 76 (84:90:98) sts. Cont in K1, P1 rib until work measures 5(5:6:6) cm/2(2:2½:2½) in from beg, ending with a right side row.
Next row Rib 11(12:9:13), * M1, rib 3(3:4:4), rep from * to last 11(12:9:13) sts, M1, rib to end. 95(105:109:117) sts.
Change to 3¼ mm/No. 4 needles. Beg with a K row cont in patt from chart. Read K rows from right to left and P rows from left to right, but work 4th row as a K row and 13th row as a P row to form ridges.
Cont in patt until work measures approx 29(32:33:35) cm/11½(12½:13:13½) in from beg, ending with an 18th (10th:10th:16th) patt row.

Shape Armholes

Keeping patt correct, cast/bind off 2 sts at beg of next 2 rows. Dec one st at each end of every row until 67 (71:77:83) sts rem. **
Cont without shaping until work measures 42(46:49:53) cm/16½(18:19¼:21) in from beg, ending with a wrong side row.

Shape Shoulders

Cast/bind off 10(10:11:12) sts at beg of next 2 rows, then 9(9:10:12) sts at beg of foll 2 rows. Leave rem 29(33:35:35) sts on a spare needle.

FRONT

Work as for Back from ** to **.
Cont without shaping until work measures 37(41:44:48) cm/14½(16:17¼:19) in from beg, ending with a wrong side row.

Shape Neck

Next row Patt 28(29:32:34) sts and turn, leaving rem sts on a spare needle, P2 tog, patt to end.
Cont on these sts only for left side of neck.
Dec one st at neck edge on every row until 19(19:21:24) sts rem.
Cont without shaping until work matches Back to shoulder, ending at armhole edge.

Shape Shoulder

Cast/bind off 10(10:11:12) sts at beg of next row.
Work 1 row.
Cast/bind off rem 9(9:10:12) sts.
With right side of work facing, return to sts on spare needle. Sl centre 11(13:13:15) sts onto a stitch holder, rejoin yarn at inner edge, patt to end.
Complete to match first side of neck.

SLEEVES

Using 2¾ mm/No. 2 needles and A, cast on 44(46:48:50) sts. Cont in K1, P1 rib until work measures 4(4:5:5) cm/1½(1½:2:2) in from beg, ending with a right side row.
Next row Rib 2(5:4:7), * M1, rib 2, rep from * to last 2(5:4:7) sts, M1, rib to end. 65(65:69:69) sts.
Change to 3¼ mm/No. 4 needles. Beg with a K row cont working patt from chart, **at the same time**, inc one st at each end of 9th(9th:5th:5th) row and every foll 10th(10th:8th:8th) row until there are 69(71:77:83) sts.
Cont without shaping until work measures approx 27(31:37:39) cm/10½(12¼:14½:15½) in from beg, ending with an 18th(10th:10th:16th) patt row.

Shape Top/Cap

Keeping patt correct, cast/bind off 2 sts at beg of next 2 rows. Now dec one st at each end of next and every foll alt row until 55(47:45:53) sts rem, ending with a wrong side row. Now dec one st at each end of every row until 23(23:25:25) sts rem. Cast/bind off.

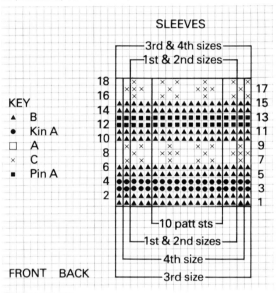

TO MAKE UP

Join right shoulder seam.

COLLAR

With right side of work facing, using 2¾ mm/No. 2 needles and A, K up 21(22:23:24) sts down left side of neck, K across 11(13:13:15) sts at centre front, inc 2 sts evenly, K up 21(22:23:24) sts up right side of neck, K across 29(33:35:35) sts on back neck, inc 4 sts evenly. 88(96:100:104) sts.
Cont in K1, P1 rib until collar measures 3 cm/1¼ in from beg, ending with a wrong side row.

Divide for Front Opening

Next row Rib 28(30:30:32) sts and turn, leaving rem sts on a spare needle.
Cont on these sts for first side. Work in K1, P1 rib for 5(6:6:7) cm/2(2½:2½:3) in. Cast/bind off in rib.
With right side of work facing, return to sts on spare needle.

1st and 2nd Sizes Only

Next row Rejoin yarn, inc in first st, rib to end. 61(67) sts.

3rd and 4th Sizes Only

Next row Rejoin yarn, work 2 tog, rib to end. (69:71) sts.

All Sizes

Complete to match first side.
Join left shoulder and collar seam, reversing seam for last 5(6:6:7) cm/2(2½:2½:3) in.
Join side and sleeve seams. Set in sleeves, easing fullness at sleeve top.

see page 17

MOVIETIME MONO

Sizes

Chest	61(66:71:76) cm	24(26:28:30) in
Length	47(50:53:56) cm	18½(19½:21:22) in
Sleeve Seam	28(29:30:32) cm	11(11½:12:12½) in

Materials

7(8:8:9) 25 g/1 oz hanks of *Rowan Yarns DK Wool* in main colour A.
4(4:5:5) hanks each in contrast colours B, C and D.
One pair each 3¼ mm/No. 4 and 4 mm/No. 6 knitting needles.
6 buttons.

Tension/gauge 25 sts and 28 rows to 10 cm/4 in over st st on 4 mm/No. 6 needles.

Abbreviations Alt-alternate; beg-beginning; cm-centimetre(s); cont-continu(e)(ing); dec-decreas(e)(ing); foll-follow(s)(ing); g-gramme(s); in-inch(es); inc-increas(e)(ing); K-knit; No.-number; oz-ounce(s); P-purl; patt-pattern; rem-remain(s)(ing); rep-repeat(ing); st(s)-stitch(es); st st-stocking stitch/stockinette stitch.

BACK

Using 3¼ mm/No. 4 needles and A, cast on 90(95:100:105) sts. Cont in K1, P1 rib as foll:
1st row (right side) K0(1:0:1), * P1, K1, rep from * to end.
2nd row * P1, K1, rep from * to last 0(1:0:1) sts, P0(1:0:1).
Rep these 2 rows until work measures 5 cm/2 in from beg, ending with a wrong side row, inc one st at each end of last row. 92(97:102:107) sts.
Change to 4 mm/No. 6 needles. Beg with a K row cont in st st working colour patt from chart. Read K rows from right to left and P rows from left to right.
Cont in patt until 72(76:80:84) rows have been worked, ending with a P row.
Shape Armholes
Dec one st at each end of next 7(5:3:3) rows, then at each end of every foll alt row until 74(81:88:95) sts rem.
Cont without shaping until 118(126:136:144) rows of patt have been worked, ending with a P row.
Shape Shoulders
Cast/bind off 23(25:27:29) sts at beg of next 2 rows.
Cast/bind off rem 28(31:34:37) sts.

LEFT FRONT

Using 3¼ mm/No. 4 needles and A, cast on 45(47:50:52) sts. Cont in K1, P1 rib as given for 2nd(2nd:1st:1st) size Back until work measures 5 cm/2 in from beg, ending with a wrong side row, inc one st at each end of last row. 47(49:52:54) sts.
Change to 4 mm/No. 6 needles. Beg with a K row cont in st st and colour patt from chart until work measures same as Back to armhole, ending with a P row.
Shape Armhole
Dec one st at armhole edge on next 7(5:3:3) rows, then dec one st at same edge on foll 2(3:4:3) alt rows. 38(41:45:48) sts.
Cont without shaping, work 14(16:20:26) rows, ending with a K row.
Shape Neck
Cast/bind off 5 sts at beg of next row, 3(3:4:4) sts at beg of 2 foll alt rows, then 2 sts at beg of next alt row. Now dec one st at beg of every foll alt row until 23(25:27:29) sts rem.
Cont without shaping until work measures same as Back to shoulder, ending with a P row.
Shape Shoulder
Cast/bind off rem sts.

RIGHT FRONT

Work as for left front, reversing all shapings.

SLEEVES

Using 3¼ mm/No. 4 needles and A, cast on 36(38:40:42) sts. Cont in K1, P1 rib until work measures 5 cm/2 in from beg, ending with a right side row.
Next row Rib 2(3:4:5), * inc in next st, rib 3, rep from * to last 2(3:4:5) sts, inc in next st, rib to end. 45(47:49:51) sts.
Change to 4 mm/No. 6 needles. Beg with a K row cont in st st and colour patt from chart, **at the same time**, inc and work into patt one st at each end of 3rd and every foll 6th row until there are 65(69:73:75) sts.
Cont without shaping, work 6(4:2:6) rows.
Shape Top/Cap
Dec one st at each end of next 3(2:1:1) rows then at each end of every foll alt row until 21(23:25:27) sts rem. Now dec one st at each end of every row until 13(15:17:15) sts rem. Cast/bind off.

BUTTONBAND

Using 3¼ mm/No. 4 needles and A, cast on 11 sts.
Cont in K1, P1 rib as given for 2nd size of Back until band, when slightly stretched, fits up left front, ending with a wrong side row. Leave sts on a safety pin.

TO MAKE UP

Sew buttonband in place. Mark the positions for 6 buttons, the first 4 rows from hem the last to be 4 rows above neck edge in neckband and the others evenly spaced between.

BUTTONHOLE BAND

Work to match buttonband, making buttonholes opposite markers as foll:

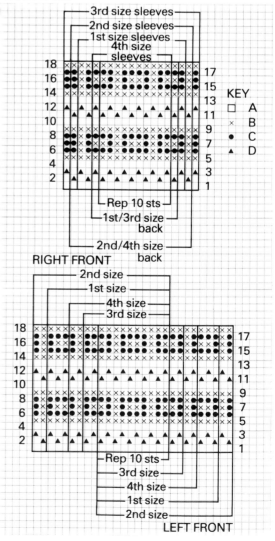

1st row (right side) Rib 4, cast/bind off 3 sts, rib to end.
2nd row Rib, casting on over those sts cast/bound off in previous row.

NECKBAND
Join shoulder seams. Sew on buttonhole band.
Using 3¼ mm/No. 4 needles and A, rib 11 sts of buttonhole band, K up 30(33:35:35) sts up right side of neck, 27(31:33:37) sts from back neck and 30(33:35:35) sts down left side of neck, then rib 11 sts of buttonband. 109(119:125:129) sts.
Beg with a wrong side row, cont in K1, P1 rib as given for 2nd size of Back.
Work 3 rows.
Now rep 1st and 2nd buttonhole rows.
Work 4 rows. Cast/bind off **loosely** in rib.
Press work lightly. Join side and sleeve seams. Set in sleeves gathering at shoulder. Sew on buttons.

see page 18

PAINTBOX BRIGHTS

Sizes
Chest	61–66(71–76) cm	24–26(28–30) in
Length	38(43) cm	15(17) in
Sleeve Seam	32(35) cm	12½(13¾) in

Materials
3(3) 50 g/2 oz balls of *Robin Reward DK* in main colour A.
2(2) balls in contrast colour B.
1(1) ball each in contrast colours C and D.
One pair each 3¼ mm/No. 4 and 4 mm/No. 6 knitting needles.

Tension/gauge 22 sts and 32 rows to 10 cm/4 in over st st on 4 mm/No. 6 needles.

Abbreviations Alt-alternate; beg-beginning; cm-centimetre(s); cont-continu(e)(ing); dec-decreas(e)(ing); foll-follow(s)(ing); g st-garter stitch; g-gramme(s); in-inch(es); inc-increas(e)(ing); K-knit; mm-millimetre(s); No.-number; oz-ounce(s); P-purl; psso-pass slipped st over; rem-remain(s)(ing); rep-repeat(ing); st st-stocking stitch/stockinette stitch; st(s)-stitch(es); sl-slip; tog-together.

BACK
Using 4 mm/No. 6 needles and A, cast on 48(52) sts **loosely**.
Form base triangles as foll:
** **1st row** (wrong side) P2, turn.
2nd row K2.
3rd row P3, turn.
4th row K3.
5th row P4, turn.
6th row K4.
7th row P5, turn.
8th row K5.
9th row P6, turn.
Cont in this way until there are 12(13) sts on right hand needle. **
Without cutting yarn rep from ** to ** 3 times more, 4 base triangles formed.
Commence First Line of Rectangles
Change to D, work a selvedge triangle as foll:
1st row K2, turn.
2nd row P2.
3rd row Inc in first st, sl 1, K1, psso, turn.
4th row P3.
5th row Inc in first st, K1, sl 1, K1, psso, turn.
6th row P4.
7th row Inc in first st, K2, sl 1, K1, psso, turn.
8th row P5.
Cont in this way until all sts of first base triangle have been used.
Leave sts on right hand needle and cont to work first rectangle as foll:
*** **1st row** K up 12(13) sts along side of base triangle.
2nd row P12(13).
3rd row K11(12), sl 1, K1, psso, turn. Two sections have been joined.
Rep last 2 rows until all sts of second base triangle have been used. ***
Rep from *** to *** using B instead of D until all sts of third base triangle have been used.
Now rep from *** to *** using D until all sts of fourth base triangle have been used.
Work a selvedge triangle as foll:

1st row K up 12(13) sts along side of fourth base triangle, turn.
2nd row P2 tog, P10(11), turn.
3rd row K11(12).
4th row P2 tog, P9(10), turn.
5th row K10(11).
Cont in this way until one st rem.
Now Work Second Line of Rectangles
**** Using A, onto needle holding last st, P up 11(12) sts along side of last triangle worked. 12(13) sts.
1st row K12(13).
2nd row P11(12), P2 tog, turn.
Rep last 2 rows until all sts of next rectangle have been worked. ****
Leave these sts on right hand needle. Rep from **** to **** 3 times more **but** P up all 12(13) sts from side of each rectangle.
Now Work Third Line of Rectangles
Work as given for first line using C instead of D.
Now Work Fourth Line of Rectangles
Work as given for second line.
Now Work Fifth Line of Rectangles
Work as given for first line.
Work Sixth Line of Rectangles
Work as given for second line.
Work Seventh Line of Rectangles
Work as given for third line.
Complete work with a line of triangles as foll:
***** Using A, P up 12(13) sts down side of last triangle worked, turn. 13(14) sts.
1st row K13(14).
2nd row P2 tog, P10(11), P2 tog, turn.
3rd row K12(13).
4th row P2 tog, P9(10), P2 tog, turn.
5th row K11(12).
6th row P2 tog, P8(9), P2 tog, turn.
Cont in this way until 3 sts rem. Work 3 tog. one st *****
Rep from ***** to ***** until 4 triangles have been worked. Fasten off rem st.

FRONT
Work as given for Back until fifth line of rectangles has been completed.
Sixth Line of Rectangles and Divide for Neck
Work as given for second line of rectangles until 2 rectangles have been completed. Cast/bind off last sts.
Now work as second line to end, completing 2 rectangles.
Seventh Line of Rectangles
Work as given for third line until first rectangle has been completed. Cast/bind off last sts.
Form Neck
Do not work across next rectangle, then work as for third line to end, so completing one rectangle and one selvedge triangle.
Complete Work with a Line of Triangles
Work triangles on shoulder sections as given for Back.

SLEEVES
Using 4 mm/No. 6 needles cast on 12(13)D, 12(13)B, 12(13)D **loosely**. 36(39) sts.
Keeping colour areas as set, work from ** to ** 3 times as given for Back.
First Line of Rectangles
Using A, work as given for first line of Back.
Second Line of Rectangles
Work as given for Back from **** to **** using C, then

rep twice more using B and C, noting to P up all 12(13) sts along sides of rectangles.

Third Line of Rectangles
Work as given for first line.

Fourth Line of Rectangles
Work as given for second line using D instead of C.

Fifth Line of Rectangles
Work as given for first line.

Sixth Line of Rectangles
Work as given for second line.
Complete work with a line of triangles as foll:
1st row Using A, K2, turn.
2nd row P2.
3rd row Inc in first st, sl 1, K1, psso.
4th row P3.
5th row Inc in first st, K1, sl 1, K1, psso, turn.
Cont in this way until 5(6) sts rem on left hand needle.
Next row P.
Cont working as set **but** now dec one st at beg of next and every foll alt row until 2(3) sts rem. Work 2(3) sts tog. One st rem.
****** K up 12(13) sts along side of next rectangle, turn. 13(14) sts.
1st row P13(14).
2nd row K2 tog, K10(11), sl 1, K1, psso, turn.
3rd row K12(13).
Cont to dec in this way until 3 sts rem. Work 3 tog. One st rem. ******

Rep from ****** to ****** once more.
K up 11(12) sts along side of last rectangle, turn. 12(13) sts.
1st row P2 tog, P10(11).
2nd row K2 tog, K9(10), turn.
Cont in this way until one st rem. Fasten off.

TO MAKE UP
Join shoulder seams.

COLLAR
Using 3¼ mm/No. 4 needles and B, cast on 12(13) sts. Cont in g st until collar is long enough, when slightly stretched, to fit around neck edge. Cast/bind off.

CUFFS
Using 3¼ mm/No. 4 needles and B, cast on 12(16) sts. Cont in g st until cuff is long enough, when slightly stretched, to fit along edge of sleeve. Cast/bind off.

WELTS
Using 3¼ mm/No. 4 needles and B, cast on 12(16) sts. Cont in g st until welt is long enough, when slightly stretched, to fit along cast on edge of work. Cast/bind off. Sew collar to neck edge, overlapping front edges to suit a boy or girl. Set in sleeves, placing centre of cast/bound off edge to shoulder seam. Sew on cuffs and welts. Join side and sleeve seams.

see page 19

COOL CABLES

Sizes

Chest	61(66:71:76) cm	24(26:28:30) in
Length	42(46:49:53) cm	16½(18:19¼:21) in
Sleeve Seam	31(35:39:43) cm	12¼(13¾:15¼:17) in

Materials
6(6:7:7) 50 g/2 oz balls of *Hayfield Raw Cotton*.
One pair each 3¼ mm/No. 4 and 4 mm/No. 6 knitting needles.
Cable needle.
3 buttons.

Tension/gauge 24 sts and 34 rows to 10 cm/4 in over patt on 4 mm/No. 6 needles.

Abbreviations Beg-beginning; cm-centimetre(s); cont-continu(e)(ing); C6F-cable 6 front, sl next 3 sts onto cable needle and hold at front of work, K3 then K3 from cable needle; dec-decreas(e)(ing); foll-follow(s)(ing); g st-garter stitch; g-gramme(s); in-inch(es); inc-increas(e)(ing); K-knit; mm-millimetre(s); M1-make one, pick up the bar that lies between st just worked and next st and work into the back of it; No.-number; oz-ounce(s); P-purl; patt-pattern; rem-remain(s)(ing); rep-repeat(ing); sl-slip; st(s)-stitch(es); yfwd/yo-yarn forward; tog-together.

CABLE PANEL—worked over 16(16:18:18) sts
1st row (right side) K.
2nd row K5(5:6:6), P6, K5(5:6:6).
3rd—4th rows Rep 1st—2nd rows.
5th row K5(5:6:6), C6F, K5(5:6:6).
6th row As 2nd row.
7th—8th rows Rep 1st—2nd rows.
These 8 rows form the cable panel.

BACK
** Using 3¼ mm/No. 4 needles, cast on 60(64:70:74) sts. Cont in K1, P1 rib until work measures 4(5:5:6) cm/ 1½(2:2:2¼) in from beg.
Next row Rib 11(4:7:9), [M1, rib 2(3:3:3)] 19 times, M1, rib to end. 80(84:90:94) sts.
Change to 4 mm/No. 6 needles and cont in patt as foll:
1st row (right side) K0(2:0:2), * work 1st row of cable panel, rep from * to last 0(2:0:2) sts, K0(2:0:2).
2nd row K0(2:0:2), * work 2nd row of cable panel, rep

from * to last 0(2:0:2) sts, K0(2:0:2).
These 2 rows establish the patt. **
Keeping cable panel correct, cont in patt as set until work measures 42:(46:49:53) cm/16½(18:19¼:21) in from beg, ending with a wrong side row.

Shape Shoulders
Cast/bind off 14(14:15:16) sts at beg of next 2 rows and 14(15:16:16) sts at beg of foll 2 rows. Leave rem 24(26:28:30) sts on a spare needle.

FRONT
Work as for Back from ** to **.
Keeping cable panel correct, cont in patt as set until work measures 30(34:36:40) cm/11¾(13¼:14¼:15¾) in from beg, ending with a wrong side row.

Divide for Neck
Next row Patt 37(39:41:43) sts and turn, leaving rem sts on a spare needle.
Cont on these sts only for left side of neck until work measures 38(41:44:48) cm/15(16:17¼:19) in from beg, ending with a wrong side row.

Shape Neck
Next row Patt 35(37:39:41) sts and turn, leaving rem 2 sts on a safety pin.
Dec one st at neck edge on every row until 28(29:31:32) sts rem.
Cont without shaping until work matches Back to shoulder, ending with a wrong side row.

Shape Shoulder
Cast/bind off 14(14:15:16) sts at beg of next row.
Work 1 row. Cast/bind off rem 14(15:16:16) sts.
With right side of work facing, return to sts on spare needle. Sl centre 6(6:8:8) sts onto a holder, rejoin yarn at inner edge and complete to match first side of neck, reversing all shapings.

SLEEVES
Using 3¼ mm/No. 4 needles, cast on 34(36:38:40) sts. Cont in K1, P1 rib until work measures 4(4:5:5) cm/ 1½(1½:2:2) in from beg.
Next row Rib 4(5:6:7), [M1, rib 2] 13 times, M1, rib to end. 48(50:52:54) sts.
Change to 4 mm/No. 6 needles and cont in patt as foll:
1st row (right side) K0 (1:2:3), * work 1st row of cable panel as for 1st size, rep from * to last 0(1:2:3) sts, K0(1:2:3).

2nd row K0(1:2:3), * work 2nd row of cable panel as for 1st size, rep from * to last 0(1:2:3) sts, K0(1:2:3).
These 2 rows establish the patt. Cont in patt, inc and work into g st, one st at each end of next and every foll 11th row until there are 60(66:70:74) sts.
Cont without shaping until work measures 31 (35:39:43) cm/12¼(13¾:15¼:17) in from beg, ending with a wrong side row. Cast/bind off **loosely**.

BUTTONBAND
*** Using 3¼ mm/No. 4 needles, cast on 9(9:11:11) sts. Cont in K1, P1 rib as foll:
1st row (right side) K1, [K1, P1] 3(3:4:4) times, K2.
2nd row K1, [P1, K1] 4(4:5:5) times.
These 2 rows form the rib. Rep the last 2 rows until band, when slightly stretched, fits up neck opening edge, ending at outer edge.
Next row Cast/bind off 4(4:5:5) sts, rib to end. ***
Break yarn and leave sts on a safety pin.
Mark the positions of 3 buttons on band. The first 3 cm/1¼ in from cast/bound off edge, the last 2 cm/1 in from neck edge and the other spaced evenly between.

BUTTONHOLE BAND
Work as for buttonband from *** to ***, **at the same time**, making buttonholes opposite markers as foll:
Buttonhole row (right side) Rib 4(4:6:6), yfwd/yo, K2 tog, rib to end.

COLLAR
Using 3¼ mm/No. 4 needle holding buttonhole band sts, and with right side of work facing, K2 sts from right neck safety pin, K up 10(12:12:14) sts up right side of neck, K across 24(26:28:30) sts at back neck inc 3 sts evenly, K up 10(12:12:14) sts down left side of neck, K2 sts from safety pin, then rib across 5(5:6:6) sts from buttonband. 61(67:71:77) sts.
Cont in K1, P1 rib until collar measures 7(7:8:8) cm/2¾(2¾:3:3) in from beg. Cast/bind off **loosely** in rib.

TO MAKE UP
Join shoulder seams.
Set in sleeves, placing centre of cast/bound off edge to shoulder seams. Join side and sleeve seams. Sew on front bands and buttons.

---

see page 20 # SLICK KNITS

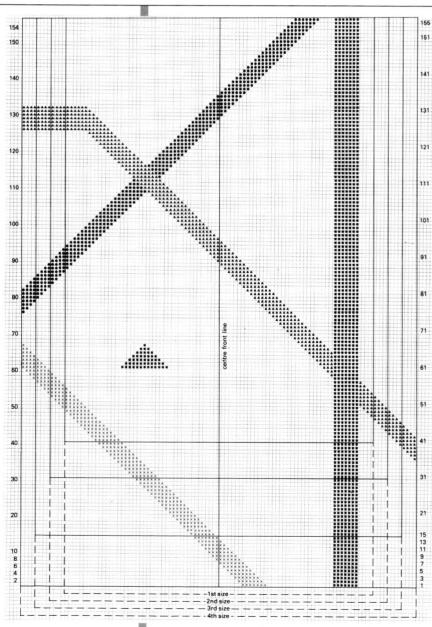

Sizes

Chest	61(66:71:76) cm	24(26:28:30) in
Length	40·5(44:50:54) cm	16(17¼:19¾:21¼) in
Sleeve Seam	30(35:40:45) cm	12(14:15¾:17¾) in

Materials
3(4:6:7) 50 g/2 oz hanks of *Rowan DK* in main colour A.
One 25 g/1 oz hank in each of 4 contrast colours B, C, D and E.
One pair each 3 mm/No. 3 and 3¾ mm/No. 5 knitting needles 4(5:6:6) buttons.

Tension/gauge
24 sts and 32 rows to 10 cm/4 in over st st using 3¾ mm/ No. 5 needles.

Abbreviations Alt-alternate; beg-beginning; cm-centimetres; cont-continu(e)(ing); dec-decreas(e)(ing); foll-follow(s)(ing); g-gramme(s); in-inch(es); inc-increas(e)(ing); K-knit; mm-millimetre(s); No.-number; oz-ounce(s); P-purl; patt-pattern; rem-remain(s)(ing); rep-repeat(ing); st(s)-stitch(es); st st-stocking stitch/stockinette stitch.

BACK
Using 3 mm/No. 3 needles and A, cast on 76(84:92:100) sts.
Cont in K1, P1 rib. Work 17(17:21:21) rows.
Next row Rib 9(10:10:11), [inc in next st, rib 7(8:9:10)] 7 times, inc in next st, rib to end. 84(92:100:108) sts.
Change to 3¾ mm/No. 5 needles. Beg with a K row, cont in st st working colour patt from chart. Use small separate balls of yarn for each colour area, twist yarns when changing colour to avoid a hole.
Commence working from 41st(31st:15th:1st) row as foll:
1st Size Only
Next row K4A, 7C, 58A, 7B, 8A.
Next row P7A, 7B, 59A, 7C, 4A.
2nd Size Only
Next row K8A, 7C, 48A, 7B, 22A.
Next row P21A, 7B, 49A, 7C, 8A.
3rd Size Only
Next row K12A, 7C, 32A, 7B, 42A.
Next row P41A, 7B, 33A, 7C, 12A.
4th Size Only
Next row K16A, 7C, 18A, 7B, 60A.
Next row P59A, 7B, 19A, 7C, 16A.
All Sizes
Cont in patt as set, reading K rows from right to left and P rows from left to right, until 154th row of chart has been worked, ending with a P row.

Shape Shoulders
Cast/bind off 28(30:32:36) sts at beg of next 2 rows.
Cast/bind off rem 28(32:36:36) sts.

LEFT FRONT
** Using 3 mm/No. 3 needles and A, cast on 38(42:46:50) sts.
Cont in K1, P1 rib. Work 17(17:21:21) rows.
Next row Rib 8(8:9:9), [inc in next st, rib 6(7:8:9)] 3 times, inc in next st, rib to end. 42(46:50:54) sts. **
Change to 3¾ mm/No. 5 needles. Beg with a K row, cont in st st working colour patt from chart between side and centre front lines and from 41st(31st:15th:1st) rows as foll:
Next row K8(22:42:54) A, 7(7:7:0) B, 27(17:1:0) A.
Next row P28(18:2:54) A, 7(7:7:0) B, 7(21:41:0) A.
Cont in patt as set, reading K rows from left to right and P rows from right to left to reverse chart.
Cont until work measures 27(29:32:35) cm/10½(11½:12½:13¾) in from beg, ending with a K row.
Shape Neck
Dec one st at neck edge on next and every foll alt row until 28(30:32:36) sts rem. Cont without shaping until 154th row of chart has been worked, ending with a P row.
Shape Shoulder
Cast/bind off rem sts.

RIGHT FRONT
Work as for left front from ** to **.
Change to 3¾ mm/No. 5 needles. Beg with a K row, cont in st st working colour patt from chart between centre front and side lines and from 41st(31st:15th:1st) row as foll:

Next row K0(0:0:6) A, 0(0:0:7) B, 31(31:31:18) A, 7C, 4(8:12:16) A.
Next row P4(8:12:16) A, 7C, 31(31:31:19) A, 0(0:0:7) B, 0(0:0:5) A.
Cont in patt as set, reading rows as for left front to reverse chart.
Complete to match left front, reversing all shapings.

LEFT SLEEVE
*** Using 3 mm/No. 3 needles and A, cast on 40(42:44:46) sts.
Cont in K1, P1 rib. Work 17(17:21:21) rows.
Next row Rib 6(7:8:3), [inc in next st, rib 1(1:1:2)] 13 times, inc in next st, rib to end. 54(56:58:60) sts. ***
Change to 3¾ mm/No. 5 needles. Cont in st st and patt as foll:
1st row K4(5:6:7) A, 5D, 36A, 5D, 4(5:6:7) A.
2nd row P4(5:6:7) A, 5D, 36A, 5D, 4(5:6:7) A.
These 2 rows establish the patt. Cont in patt as set, **at the same time**, inc and work into st st and A, one st at each end of foll 3rd then every foll 4th row until there are 84(96:84:90) sts.
3rd and 4th Sizes Only
Cont to inc one st at each end of every foll 3rd row until there are (108:120) sts.
All Sizes
Cont without shaping. Work 18(14:18:17) rows.
Cast/bind off **loosely**.

RIGHT SLEEVE
Work as for left sleeve from *** to ***.
Change to 3¾ mm/No. 5 needles. Beg with a K row cont in st st as given for left sleeve but working colour patt from chart, reading rows as for Back.

TO MAKE UP
Press lightly, omitting ribbing. Join shoulder seams.

FRONTBAND
Using 3 mm/No. 3 needles and A, cast on 9(9:11:11) sts.
Cont in K1, P1 rib as foll:
1st row K1, * P1, K1, rep from * to end.
2nd row P1, * K1, P1, rep from * to end.
Rep last 2 rows once more.
1st buttonhole row Rib 4(4:5:5), cast/bind off 2 sts, rib to end.
2nd buttonhole row Rib to end, casting on 2 sts over those cast/bound off in previous row.
Cont in rib as set until band is long enough, when slightly stretched, to fit up front edge, across back neck and down front edge, **at the same time**, making 3(4:5:5) more buttonholes at intervals of 8(7:6:6·5) cm/3¼(3:2¼:2½) in measured from base of previous buttonhole.
Cast/bind off in rib.
Set in sleeves, placing centre of cast/bound off edge to shoulder seam. Join side and sleeve seams. Sew on frontband. Sew on buttons.

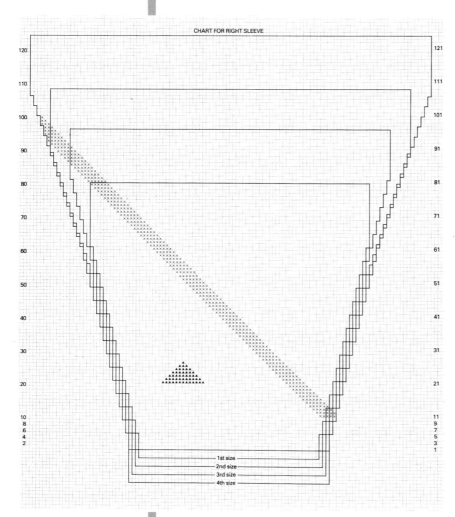

CHART FOR RIGHT SLEEVE

see page 22

BRIGHT SPARK

Sizes

Chest	61(66:71:76) cm	24(26:28:30) in
Length	45(50:53:58) cm	17¾(19½:21:23) in
Sleeve Seam	27(32:37:38) cm	10½(12½:14½:15) in

Materials

7(7:8:8) 50 g/2 oz balls of *Argyll Cocktail* in main colour A.

2(2:3:3) 50 g/2 oz balls of *Argyll Nice 'n' Easy Double Crepe* in contrast colour B.

1(1:2:2) balls in contrast colour C.

One pair each 3¼ mm/No. 4, 4 mm/No. 6 and 5½ mm/No. 9 knitting needles.

Tension/gauge 20 sts and 22 rows to 10 cm/4 in over st st on 5½ mm/No. 9 needles.

> **Abbreviations** Alt-alternate; beg-beginning; cm-centimetre(s); cont-continu(e)(ing); dec-decrease(e)(ing); foll-follow(s)(ing); g-gramme(s); in-inch(es); inc-increas(e)(ing); K-knit; mm-millimetre(s); No.-number; oz-ounce(s); P-purl; patt-pattern; rem-remain(s)(ing); rep-repeat(ing); st st-stocking stitch/stockinette stitch; st(s)-stitch(es); sl-slip; tog-together.

BACK

** Using 3¼ mm/No. 4 needles and B, cast on 67(73:77:83) sts. Cont in K1, P1 rib as foll:

1st row (right side) K1, * P1, K1, rep from * to end.

2nd row P1, * K1, P1, rep from * to end.

Rep these 2 rows until work measures 5 cm/2 in from beg, ending with a right side row.

Next row Rib 7(12:8:14) inc in next st, * rib 12(23:14:26), inc in next st, rep from * to last 7(12:8:14) sts, rib to end. 72(76:82:86) sts.

Change to 5½ mm/No. 9 needles. Beg with a K row cont in st st working colour patt from chart. Read K rows from right to left and P rows from left to right. Strand yarn not in use **loosely** across back of work. **

Cont until work measures 45(50:53:58) cm/17¾(19½:21:23) in from beg, ending with a P row.

Shape Shoulders

Cast/bind off 24(25:28:29) sts at beg of next 2 rows. Leave rem 24(26:26:28) sts on a spare needle.

FRONT

Work as given for Back from ** to **.

Cont until work measures 14 rows less than Back to shoulder, ending with a P row.

Shape Neck

Next row Patt 28(29:32:33), work 2 tog and turn, leaving rem sts on a spare needle.

Complete left side of neck first.

Dec one st at neck edge on next 2 rows then at same edge on foll 3 alt rows. 24(25:28:29) sts.

Cont without shaping until work measures same as Back to shoulder, ending at armhole edge.

Shape Shoulder

Cast/bind off rem sts.

With right side of work facing, return to sts on spare needle. Sl centre 12(14:14:16) sts onto a stitch holder, rejoin yarn at neck edge, work 2 tog, patt to end.

Complete to match first side of neck.

SLEEVES

Using 3¼ mm/No. 4 needles and B, cast on 39(41:41:41) sts. Cont in K1, P1, rib as given for Back until work measures 5 cm/2 in from beg, ending with a right side row.

Next row Rib 3(4:2:2), inc in next st, * rib 1, inc in next st, rep from * to last 3(4:2:2) sts, rib to end. 56(58:60:60) sts.

Change to 5½ mm/No. 9 needles. Beg with a K row cont in st st working colour patt from chart, **at the same time**, inc one st at each end of 1st and every foll 4th(5th:7th:6th) row until there are 72(76:76:80) sts.

Cont without shaping until work measures 24(29:34:35) cm/9½(11½:13½:13¾) in from beg, ending with a P row.

Change to 4 mm/No. 6 needles and cont in B only.

Next row K5(4:4:3), inc in next st, * K9(10:10:8), inc in next st, rep from * to last 6(5:5:4) sts, K to end. 79(83:83:89) sts.

Cont in K1, P1 rib as given for Back, beg with a wrong side row, until work measures 27(32:37:38) cm/10½(12½:14½:15) in from beg. Cast/bind off **loosely** in rib.

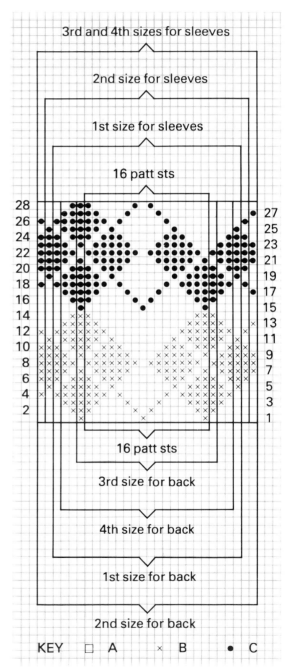

3rd and 4th sizes for sleeves

2nd size for sleeves

1st size for sleeves

16 patt sts

16 patt sts

3rd size for back

4th size for back

1st size for back

2nd size for back

KEY   □ A   × B   • C

TO MAKE UP
Join right shoulder seam.

NECKBAND
With right side of work facing, using 3¼ mm/No. 4 needles and B, K up 14 sts down left side of neck, K across 12(14:14:16) sts at centre front inc one st, K up 14 sts up right side of neck, K across 24(26:26:28) sts at back neck inc 2 sts evenly. 67(71:71:75) sts.
Cont in K1, P1 rib as given for Back until neckband measures 5 cm/2 in from beg. Cast/bind off **very loosely** in rib.
Join left shoulder and neckband. Fold neckband in half onto wrong side and catch down.
Set in sleeves, placing centre of cast/bound off edge to shoulder seam. Join side and sleeve seams.

see page 23

STRIKER

Sizes

Chest	61(66:71:76) cm	24(26:28:30) in
Length	42(46:49:51) cm	16½(18:19¼:20) in
Sleeve Seam	29(33:37:41) cm	11½(13:14½:16) in

Materials
Sweater
8(8:9:10) 50 g/2 oz balls of *Pingouin Naturelle Sport*.
One pair each 3¾ mm/No. 5 and 4½ mm/No. 7 knitting needles.
Cable needle.
4 buttons.

Tension/gauge 23 sts and 31 rows to 10 cm/4 in over patt on 4½ mm/No. 7 needles.

Abbreviations Alt-alternate; beg-beginning; cm-centimetre(s); cont-continu(e)(ing); dec-decreas(e)(ing); foll-follow(s)(ing); g-gramme(s); g st-garter stitch; in-inch(es); inc-increas(e)(ing); K-knit; KB-sl next st onto cable needle and hold at back of work, K2, then P1 from cable needle; LC-sl next 2 sts onto cable needle and hold at front of work, K1 then K2 from cable needle; LCF-sl next 2 sts onto cable needle and hold at front of work, P1 then K2 from cable needle; LCP-sl next 2 sts onto cable needle and hold at back of work, P1 then P2 from cable needle; mm-millimetre(s); No.-number; oz-ounce(s); P-purl; patt-pattern; PB-sl next 2 sts onto cable needle and hold at back of work, K1 then P2 from cable needle; psso-pass slipped st over; rem-remain(s)(ing); rep-repeat(ing); rev st st-reverse stocking stitch/stockinette stitch; RC-sl next st onto cable needle and hold at back of work, K2, then K1 from cable needle; RCF- sl next st onto cable needle and hold at front of work, P2 then K1 from cable needle; RCP-sl next st onto cable needle and hold at front of work, P2 then P1 from cable needle; st(s)-stitch(es); sl-slip; tog-together.

PATT PANEL A (worked over 28 sts)
1st row (right side) P4, RC, LC, P8, RC, LCF, P4.
2nd row K3, RCF, P1, K1, LCP, K6, RCP, P2, LCP, K3.
3rd row P2, RC, K4, LC, P4, RC, [P1, K1] twice, LCF, P2.
4th row K1, RCF, [P1, K1] 3 times, LCP, K2, RCP, P6, LCP, K1.
5th row P1, K12, P2, K2, [P1, K1] 4 times, K2, P1.
6th row K1, P2, [K1, P1] 4 times, P2, K2, P12, K1.
7th–12th rows Rep 5th–6th rows 3 times.
13th row P1, LCF, K6, KB, P2, LCF, [K1, P1] 3 times, KB, P1.
14th row K2, PB, [K1, P1] twice, RCF, K4, PB, P4, RCF, K2.
15th row P3, LCF, K2, KB, P6, LCF, K1, P1, KB, P3.
16th row K4, PB, RCF, K8, PB, RCF, K4.
17th row P4, RC, LCF, P8, RC, LC, P4.
18th row K3, RCP, P2, LCP, K6, RCF, P1, K1, LCP, K3.
19th row P2, RC, [P1, K1] twice, LCF, P4, RC, K4, LC, P2.
20th row K1, RCP, P6, LCP, K2, RCF, [P1, K1] 3 times, LCP, K1.
21st row P1, K2, [P1, K1] 4 times, K2, P2, K12, P1.
22nd row K1, P12, K2, P2, [K1, P1] 4 times, P2, K1.
23rd–28th rows Rep 21st–22nd rows 3 times.
29th row P1, LCF, [K1, P1] 3 times, KB, P2, LCF, K6, KB, P1.
30th row K2, PB, P4, RCF, K4, PB, [K1, P1] twice, RCF, K2.
31st row P3, LCF, K1, P1, KB, P6, LCF, K2, KB, P3.
32nd row K4, PB, RCF, K8, PB, RCF, K4.
These 32 rows form patt panel A.

PATT PANEL B (worked over 14 sts)
1st row (right side) P4, RC, LC, P4.
2nd row K3, RCP, P2, LCP, K3.
3rd row P2, RC, K4, LC, P2.
4th row K1, RCP, P6, LCP, K1.
5th row P1, K12, P1.
6th row K1, P12, K1.
7th–12th rows Rep 5th–6th rows 3 times.
13th row P1, LCF, K6, KB, P1.
14th row K2, PB, P4, RCF, K2.
15th row P3, LCF, K2, KB, P3.
16th row K4, PB, RCF, K4.
17th row P4, RC, LCF, P4.
18th row K3, RCP, P2, LCP, K3.
19th row P2, RC, [P1, K1] twice, LCF, P2.
20th row K1, RCF, [P1, K1] 3 times, LCP, K1.
21st row P1, K2, [P1, K1] 4 times, K2, P1.
22nd row K1, P2, [K1, P1] 4 times, P2, K1.
23rd–28th rows Rep 21st–22nd rows 3 times.
29th row P1, LCF, [K1, P1] 3 times, KB, P1.
30th row K2, PB, [K1, P1] twice, RCF, K2.
31st row P3, LCF, K1, P1, KB, P3.
32nd row K4, PB, RCF, K4.
These 32 rows form patt panel B.

BACK
** Using 3¾ mm/No. 5 needles, cast on 64(70:76:84) sts.
Cont in K2, P2 rib as foll:
1st row (right side) K0(2:0:0), * P2, K2, rep from * to end.
2nd row * P2, K2, rep from * to last 0(2:0:0) sts, P0(2:0:0).
Rep these 2 rows until work measures 5(6:6:7) cm/2(2½:2½:2¾) in from beg, ending with a right side row.
Next row Rib 3(6:9:4), * inc in next st, rib 2(2:2:3), rep from * to last 4(7:10:4) sts, inc in next st, rib to end. 84(90:96:104) sts.
Change to 4½ mm/No. 7 needles and cont in patt as foll:
1st row (right side) P0(3:6:3), [work 1st row patt panel A] 3 times, [work 1st row patt panel B] 0(0:0:1) time, P0(3:6:3).
2nd row K0(3:6:3), [work 2nd row patt panel B] 0(0:0:1) time, [work 2nd row patt panel A] 3 times, K0(3:6:3).
These 2 rows establish the patt, placing patt panels and edge sts in rev st st. **
Keeping patt correct, cont until work measures 42(46:49:51) cm/16½(18:19¼:20) in from beg, ending with a wrong side row.
Shape Shoulders
Cast/bind off 14(15:16:17) sts at beg of next 4 rows.
Leave rem 28(30:32:36) sts on a spare needle.

FRONT
Work as given for Back from ** to **.
Keeping patt correct, cont until work measures 38(41:44:46) cm/15(16¼:17½:18) in from beg, ending with a wrong side row.
Shape Neck
Next row Patt 35(37:40:43) sts and turn leaving rem sts on a spare needle.

Complete left side of neck first.
Dec one st at neck edge on every row until 28(30:32:34) sts rem.
Cont without shaping until work measures same as Back to shoulder, ending at armhole edge.

Shape Shoulder
Cast/bind off 14(15:16:17) sts at beg of next row. Work 1 row. Cast/bind off rem 14(15:16:17) sts.
With right side of work facing, return to sts on spare needle. Sl centre 14(16:16:18) sts onto a stitch holder, rejoin yarn at neck edge, patt to end. Complete to match first side of neck.

SLEEVES
Using 3¾ mm/No. 5 needles, cast on 26(28:30:32) sts.
Cont in K2, P2 rib as given for 2nd(1st:2nd:1st) size of Back until work measures 4(4:5:5) cm/1½(1½:2:2) in from beg, ending with a right side row.
Next row Rib 3(0:2:3), * inc in next st, rep from * to last 3(0:2:3) sts, rib to end. 46(56:56:58) sts.
Change to 4½ mm/No. 7 needles and cont in patt as foll:
1st row (right side) P2(0:0:1), [work 17th row patt panel B] 1(0:0:0) time, [work 17th row patt panel A] 1(2:2:2) times, P2(0:0:1).
2nd row K2(0:0:1), [work 18th row patt panel A] 1(2:2:2) times, [work 18th row patt panel B] 1(0:0:0) times, K2(0:0:1).
These 2 rows establish the patt, placing patt panels and edge sts.
Cont, keeping patt correct, **at the same time**, inc and work into rev st st, one st at each end of 3rd and every foll 4th row until there are 64(70:74:78) sts.
Cont without shaping until work measures 29(33:37:41) cm/11½(13:14½:16) in from beg, ending with a wrong side row. Cast/bind off **loosely**.

TO MAKE UP
Join right shoulder seam.

NECKBAND
With right side of work facing, using 3¾ mm/No. 5 needles, K up 12(13:14:14) sts down left side of neck, K across 14(16:16:18) sts at centre front, K up 12(13:14:14) sts up left side of neck, then K across 28(30:32:36) sts at back neck. 66(72:76:82) sts.
Cont in K2, P2 rib as given for 2nd(1st:1st:2nd) size of Back until neckband measures 3(4:4:4) cm/1¼(1½:1½:1½) in from beg. Cast/bind off **loosely** in rib.

BUTTONBAND
With right side of work facing, using 3¾ mm/No. 5 needles, K up 36(40:42:46) sts from left back shoulder.
Cont in K2, P2 rib as given for 1st(1st:2nd:2nd) size Back until band measures 2(3:3:3) cm/¾(1¼:1¼:1¼) in from beg. Cast/bind off in rib.

BUTTONHOLE BAND
With right side of work facing, using 3¾ mm/No. 5 needles, K up 36(40:42:46) sts from left front shoulder.
Cont in K2, P2 rib as given for buttonband until band measures 1 cm/½ in from beg, ending with a wrong side row.
Next row Rib 4(4:5:6), * cast/bind off one, rib 8(9:9:10) including st used to cast/bind off, rep from * twice more, cast/bind off one, rib to end.
Next row Rib casting on one st over that cast/bound off in previous row.
Complete to match buttonband.
Catch ends of bands together at armhole edge. Set in sleeves placing centre of cast/bound off edge to shoulder seam. Join side and sleeve seams. Sew on buttons.

---

see page 24

FAIR ISLE RAMBLER

Sizes
Chest	61(66:71:76) cm	24(26:28:30) in
Length	40(44:48:52) cm	16(17½:19:20½) in
Sleeve Seam	31(35:39:43) cm	12¼(13¾:15½:17) in

Materials
3(3:4:4) 50 g/2 oz balls of *Patons Clansman Superwash* 4 ply in main colour A.
2(2:3:3) balls in contrast colour B.
1(1:1:1) ball each in contrast colours C, D and E.
One pair each 2¾ mm/No. 2 and 3¼ mm/No. 4 knitting needles.
2 buttons.

Tension/gauge 32 sts and 32 rows to 10 cm/4 in over patt on 3¼ mm/No. 4 needles.

Abbreviations Alt-alternate; beg-beginning; cm-centimetre(s); cont-continu(e)(ing); dec-decrease(e)(ing); foll-follow(s)(ing); g-gramme(s); in-inch(es); inc-increas(e)(ing); K-knit; mm-millimetre(s); M1-make one by picking up the bar that lies between the st just worked and next st and working into the back of it; No.-number; oz-ounce(s); P-purl; patt-pattern; rem-remain(s)(ing); rep-repeat(ing); st st-stocking stitch/stockinette stitch; sl-slip; st(s)-stitch(es).

BACK
** Using 2¾ mm/No. 2 needles and A, cast on 84(94:100:108) sts. Cont in K1, P1 rib until work measures 5(5:6:6) cm/2(2:2½:2½) in from beg, ending with a right side row.
Next row Rib 6(11:2:6), * M1, rib 3(3:4:4), rep from * to last 6(11:2:6) sts, M1, rib to end. 109(119:125:133) sts.
Change to 3¼ mm/No. 4 needles. Beg with a K row cont in st st working colour patt from chart, reading K rows from right to left and P rows from left to right. **

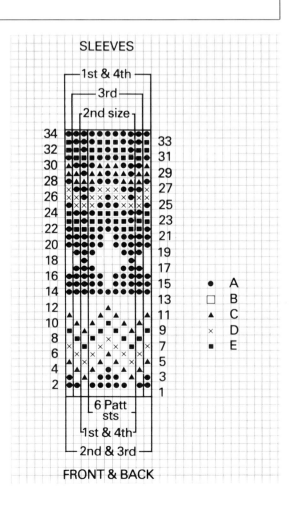

SLEEVES

1st & 4th
3rd
2nd size

6 Patt sts
1st & 4th
2nd & 3rd

FRONT & BACK

- ● A
- □ B
- ▲ C
- × D
- ■ E

Cont in patt until work measures 40(44:48:52) cm/16(17½:19:20½) in from beg, ending with a P row.
Shape Shoulders
Cast/bind off 18(20:22:23) sts at beg of next 2 rows and 19(21:21:23) sts at beg of foll 2 rows. Leave rem 35(37:39:41) sts on a spare needle.

FRONT
Work as given for Back from ** to **.
Cont in patt until work measures 32(35:38:42) cm/12¾(13¾:15:16½) in from beg, ending with a P row.
Divide for front opening.
Next row Patt 51(56:58:62) sts and turn, leaving rem sts on a spare needle. Complete left side of neck first.
Cont in patt until work measures 35(39:43:47) cm/13¾(15½:17:18½) in from beg, ending at side edge.
Shape Neck
Next row Patt 45(50:52:56) sts and turn, leaving rem 6 sts on a safety pin.
Dec one st at neck edge on every row until 37(41:43:46) sts rem.
Cont without shaping until work measures same as Back to shoulder, ending at armhole edge.
Shape Shoulder
Cast/bind off 18(20:22:23) sts at beg of next row. Work 1 row. Cast/bind off rem 19(21:21:23) sts.
With right side of work facing, return to sts on spare needle. Sl centre 7(7:9:9) sts onto a stitch holder, rejoin yarn at neck edge, patt to end.
Cont until work measures same as left side to neck, ending at side edge.
Shape Neck
Next row Patt to last 6 sts, turn, leave these sts on a safety pin.
Complete to match left side of neck.

SLEEVES
Using 2¾ mm/No. 2 needles and A, cast on 44(46:48:50) sts. Cont in K1, P1 rib until work measures 4(4:5:5) cm/1½(1½:2:2) in from beg, ending with a right side row.
Next row Rib 2(3:4:5), * M1, rib 2, rep from * to last 2(3:4:5) sts, M1, rib to end. 65(67:69:71) sts.
Change to 3¼ mm/No. 4 needles. Beg with a K row cont in st st working colour patt from chart, **at the same time**, inc one st at each end of 3rd and every foll 6th row until there are 89(95:101:107) sts.

Cont without shaping until work measures 31 (35:39:43) cm/12¼(13¾:15½:17) in from beg, ending with a P row. Cast/bind off **loosely**.

TO MAKE UP
Join shoulder seams.

BUTTONBAND
Using 2¾ mm/No. 2 needles and A, cast on 9(9:11:11) sts.
1st row (right side) K2, * P1, K1, rep from * to last st, K1.
2nd row K1, * P1, K1, rep from * to end.
Rep these 2 rows until band is long enough, when slightly stretched, to fit up opening edge of front to neck, ending with a wrong side row. Leave sts on a safety pin.

BUTTONHOLE BAND
Mark positions for 2 buttons on buttonband, one 2 cm/¾ in from base, the other 2 rows from neck.
With right side of work facing, using 2¾ mm/No. 2 needles and A, K up 7(7:9:9) sts from centre front, inc 2 sts evenly. 9(9:11:11) sts.
Cont in rib as given for buttonband, beg with a wrong side row, **at the same time**, making buttonholes opposite markers as foll:
1st row (right side) Rib 4(4:5:5) sts, cast/bind off one st, rib to end.
2nd row Rib to end, casting on one st over that cast/bound off in previous row. Cont in rib until band measures same as buttonband, ending with a wrong side row. Do not break yarn.

COLLAR
With right side of work facing, using 2¾ mm/No. 2 needles and A, rib sts of buttonhole band, K6 sts on pin K up 22(22:23:23) sts up right side of neck, K across 35(37:39:41) sts at Back neck, K up 22(22:23:23) sts down left side of neck, K6 sts on pin, rib across sts of buttonband. 109(111:119:121) sts.
Cont in rib as set, work 3 rows.
Cast/bind off 6 sts at beg of next 2 rows. Cont in rib until collar measures 6(7:7:8) cm/2½(2¾:2¾:3) in from beg. Cast/bind off **loosely** in rib.
Set in sleeves, placing centre of cast/bound off edge to shoulder seam. Join side and sleeve seams. Sew on buttons.

see page 25 # HIKER'S HANDKNIT

Sizes

Chest	61(66:71:76) cm	24(26:28:30) in
Length	39(43:48:53) cm	15½(17:19:21) in
Sleeve Seam	26·5(32:37:38) cm	10½(12½:14½:15) in

Materials
3(3:4:5) 50 g/2 oz hanks of *Rowan DK* in main colour A.
One 25 g/1 oz hank in each of 4 contrast colours (B, C, D and E).
One pair each 3 mm/No. 3 and 3¾ mm/No. 5 knitting needles.
8(8:9:9) buttons.

Tension/gauge 26 sts and 34 rows to 10 cm/4 in over spot patt using 3¾ mm/No. 5 needles.

Abbreviations Alt-alternate; approx-approximately; beg-beginning; cm-centimetre(s); cont-continu(e)(ing); dec-decreas(e)(ing); foll-follow(s)(ing); g-gramme(s); in-inch(es); inc-increase(e)(ing); K-knit; mm-millimetre(s); No.-number; oz-ounce(s); P-purl; patt-pattern; rem-remain(s)(ing); rep-repeat(ing); sl-slip; st(s)-stitch(es); st st-stocking stitch/stockinette stitch; tbl-through back of loop(s).

BACK AND FRONTS—worked in one piece to underarm
Using 3 mm/No. 3 needles and E, cast on 172(184:196:208) sts.

Change to A and cont in K1, P1 rib. Work 4 rows.
1st buttonhole row (right side) Rib 4, cast/bind off 2 sts, work to end.
2nd buttonhole row Work to end, casting on 2 sts over those cast/bound off in previous row.
Work 11 rows.
Next row Rib 14(20:21:21), [inc 1, rib 12(12:13:14)] 11 times, inc 1, rib to end. 184(196:208:220) sts.
Change to 3¾ mm/No. 5 needles.
Next row Rib 8, K to last 8 sts, rib 8.
Next row Rib 8, P to last 8 sts, rib 8.
These 2 rows establish the front borders in rib. Keeping borders in rib, commence spot patt, **at the same time**, making 6(6:7:7) more buttonholes as before at intervals of 5(5·5:5:6) cm/2(2¼:2:2½) in measured from base of previous buttonhole. Join in contrast colours as required within the front borders and strand yarn not in use **loosely** across back of work.
1st row (right side) Using A, rib 8, K2(4:2:4) A, * 1B, 3A, rep from * to last 10(12:10:12) sts, 1B, 1(3:1:3) A, using A, rib 8.
2nd row Using A, rib 8, P1(3:1:3), * K1 tbl, P3, rep from * to last 11(13:11:13) sts, K1 tbl, P2(4:2:4), rib 8.
3rd row Using A, rib 8, K to last 8 sts, rib 8.
4th row Using A, rib 8, P to last 8 sts, rib 8.
5th row Using A, rib 8, K4(2:4:2) A, * 1C, 3A, rep from * to last 12(10:12:10) sts, 1C, 3(1:3:1) A, using A, rib 8.
6th row Using A, rib 8, P3(1:3:1), * K1 tbl, P3, rep from * to last 13(11:13:11) sts, K1 tbl, P4(2:4:2), rib 8.
7th row As 3rd row.

8th row As 4th row.

9th row As 1st row **but** using D instead of B.

10th row As 2nd row.

11th row As 3rd row.

12th row As 4th row.

13th row As 5th row **but** using E instead of C.

14th row As 6th row.

15th row As 3rd row.

16th row As 4th row.

These 16 rows form the spot patt with rib front borders. Rep these 16 rows until work measures 24(25·5:28:30·5) cm/9½(10:11:12) in from beg, ending with a wrong side row.

Divide for Armholes

Next row Rib 8, patt 40(43:46:49), cast/bind off 4 sts, patt 80(86:92:98) including st used in casting/binding off, cast/bind off 4 sts, work to end.

Cont on last 48(50:54:57) sts for left front.

Cont as set, keeping patt correct until work measures 26·5(28:30·5:33) cm/10½(11:12:13) in approx from beg ending with an 8th(12th:4th:12th) patt row. Commence colour patt from appropriate chart. Read odd numbered rows as K rows from right to left and even numbered rows as P rows from left to right.

Next row Work 40(43:46:49) sts as 1st row of chart, using A, rib 8.

Next row Using A, rib 8, work 40(43:46:49) sts as 2nd row of chart.

Cont in this way until work measures 33·5(36·5:40·5:44·5) cm/13(14½:16:17½) in from beg, ending at front edge.

Shape Neck

Next row Using A, rib 8 and sl these sts onto a safety pin, cast/bind off 6 sts, work to end.

Keeping patt correct, cast/bind off 2 sts at beg of foll 3 alt rows then dec one st at beg of every foll alt row until 27(28:30:32) sts rem.

Now cont without shaping until work measures 39(43:48:53) cm/15½(17:19:21) in from beg, ending at armhole edge.

Cast/bind off these rem sts.

With wrong side of work facing return to 80(86:92:98) sts for Back.

Keeping patt correct, cont until work measures 26·5(28:30·5:33) cm/10½(11:12:13) in approx from beg, ending with an 8th(12th:4th:12th) patt row.

Now commence colour patt from chart and cont until work matches left front to shoulder.

Cast/bind off 27(28:30:32) sts at beg of next 2 rows. Leave the rem 26(30:32:34) sts on a holder.

With wrong side of work facing, return to 48(50:54:57) sts for right front. Cont as set, keeping patt correct and making buttonholes until work measures 26·5(28:30·5:33) cm/10½(11:12:13) in approx from beg, ending with an 8th(12th:4th:12th) patt row. Commence colour patt from chart.

Next row Using A, rib 8, work 40(43:46:49) sts as 1st row of chart.

Next row Work 40(43:46:49) sts as 2nd row of chart, using A, rib 8.

Complete to match left front.

SLEEVES

Using 3 mm/No. 3 needles and E, cast on 40(42:44:46) sts.

Change to A and cont in K1, P1 rib. Work 17 rows.

Next row Rib 6(7:8:3), [inc 1, rib 1(1:1:2)] 13 times, inc 1, rib to end. 54(56:58:60) sts.

Change to 3¾ mm/No. 5 needles and beg with a K row work 4 rows st st.

Now commence spot patt.

1st row (right side) K2(3:4:5) A, * 1B, 3A, rep from * to last 4(5:6:7) sts, 1B, 3(4:5:6) A.

This row establishes the spot patt as given for Back. Cont in patt, inc one st at each end of the next and every foll 4th row until there are 78(92:104:112) sts.

Cont without shaping until sleeve measures 26·5(32:37:38) cm/10½(12½:14½:15) in from beg, ending with a wrong side row. Cast off **loosely**.

TO MAKE UP

Join shoulder seams.

COLLAR

With right side of work facing, sl the 8 sts off right front safety pin onto a 3 mm/No. 3 needle, join in A at inner neck edge, K up 29(29:35:35) sts up right side of neck, K across 26(30:32:34) sts from back neck holder, K up 29(29:35:35) sts down left side of neck, then rib across 8 sts on safety pin. 100(104:118:120) sts.

Cont in K1, P1 rib. Work 5 rows then work 1st and 2nd buttonhole rows as given for Back.

Work 2 rows.

Change to 3¾ mm/No. 5 needles and cont in rib until collar measures 7(9:10:10) cm/2¾(3½:4:4) in from beg.

Change to E and cast/bind off fairly **loosely**.

Press lightly omitting ribbing. Set sleeves into armholes, matching the centre of cast/bound off edge to shoulder seam. Join sleeve seams. Sew on buttons.

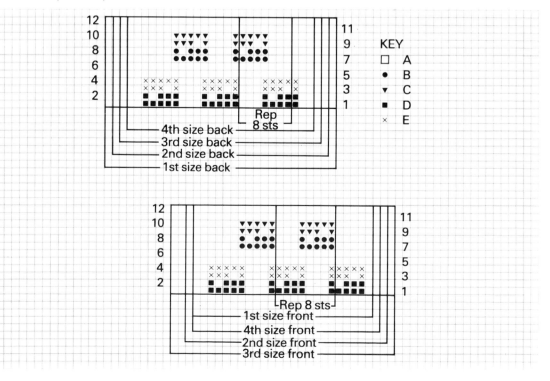

see page 26

MELLOW MELODY

see page 26
see page 27

Sizes

Chest	61(66:71:76) cm	24(26:28:30) in
Length	40(45:48:52) cm	16(17¾:19:20½) in
Sleeve Seam	28(32:36:39) cm	11(12½:14:15½) in

Materials

7(8:8:9) 50 g/2 oz balls of *Emu Superwash DK*.
One pair each 3¼ mm/No. 4 and 4 mm/No. 6 knitting needles.
3¼ mm/No. 4 circular needle.
Cable needle.

Tension/gauge 22 sts and 31 rows to 10 cm/4 in over moss st patt on 4 mm/No. 6 needles.

Abbreviations Alt-alternate; beg-beginning; C3L-sl next 2 sts onto cable needle and hold at front of work, P1, then K2 from cable needle; C3R-sl next st onto cable needle and hold at back of work, K2 then P1 from cable needle; C4B-sl next 2 sts onto cable needle and hold at back of work, K2 then K2 from cable needle; C4F-sl next 2 sts onto cable needle and hold at front of work, K2 then K2 from cable needle; cm-centimetre(s); cont-continu(e)(ing); dec-decreas(e)(ing); foll-follow(s)(ing); g-gramme(s); in-inch(es); inc-increas(e)(ing); K-knit; No.-number; oz-ounce(s); P-purl; patt-pattern; rem-remain(s)(ing); rep-repeat(ing); st(s)-stitch(es); sl-slip; tog-together.

CABLE PANEL A (worked over 14 sts)

1st row (wrong side) [K2, P4] twice, K2.
2nd row [P2, C4F] twice, P2.
3rd row As 1st row.
4th row [P2, K4] twice, P2.
These 4 rows form the patt for cable panel A.

CABLE PANEL B (worked over 20 sts)

1st row (wrong side) K4, [P4, K4] twice.
2nd row P4, C4B, P4, C4F, P4.
3rd and every foll alt row K the P sts and P the K sts of previous row.
4th row P3, C3R, C3L, P2, C3R, C3L, P3.
6th row P2, [C3R, P2, C3L] twice, P2.
8th row P2, K2, P4, C4B, P4, K2, P2.
10th row P2, K2, P4, K4, P4, K2, P2.
12th row As 8th row.
14th row P2, [C3L, P2, C3R] twice, P2.
16th row P3, C3L, C3R, P2, C3L, C3R, P3.
18th row As 2nd row.
20th row As 4th row.
22nd row P3, [K2, P2] twice, K2, sl last 6 sts just worked onto cable needle, wrap yarn 4 times anti-clockwise round these 6 sts, then sl them back onto right hand needle, P2, K2, P3.
These 22 rows form the patt for cable panel B.

BACK

** Using 3¼ mm/No. 4 needles, cast on 78(82:90:94) sts.
Cont in K1, P1 rib until work measures 5 cm/2 in from beg, ending with a wrong side row.
Next row Rib 0(2:6:8), * inc in next st, rib 3, rep from * to last 2(4:8:10) sts, inc in next st, rib to end. 98(102:110:114) sts.
Change to 4 mm/No. 6 needles and cont in patt as foll:
1st row (wrong side) K1, [P1, K1] 7(8:10:11) times, work 1st row cable panel A, [work 1st row cable panel B] twice, work 1st row cable panel A, K1, [P1, K1] 7(8:10:11) times.
2nd row K1, [P1, K1] 7(8:10:11) times, work 2nd row cable panel A, [work 2nd row cable panel B] twice, work 1st row cable panel A, K1, [P1, K1] 7(8:10:11) times.
These 2 rows establish the patt, placing cable panels and edge sts in moss st patt. ** Keeping panels correct cont until work measures 40(45:48:52) cm/16(17¾:19:20½) in from beg, ending with a wrong side row.

Shape Shoulders

Next row Cast/bind off 33(34:36:37) sts, patt 32(34:38:40) including st used to cast/bind off, cast/bind off rem sts. Leave sts on a spare needle.

FRONT

Work as given for Back from ** to **.
Keeping panels correct cont until work measures 33(36:39:43) cm/13(14:15½:17) in from beg, ending with a wrong side row.

Shape Neck

Next row Patt 39(40:43:44) sts and turn, leaving rem sts on a spare needle.
Complete left side of neck first.
Dec one st at neck edge on every row until 33(34:36:37) sts rem.
Cont without shaping until work measures same as Back to shoulder, ending with a wrong side row.

Shape Shoulder

Cast/bind off rem sts.
With right side of work facing, return to sts on spare needle. Sl centre 20(22:24:26) sts onto a stitch holder, rejoin yarn at neck edge, patt to end.
Complete to match first side of neck.

SLEEVES

Using 3¼ mm/No. 4 needles, cast on 40(42:44:48) sts.
Cont in K1, P1 rib until work measures 4(6:6:6) cm/1½(2½:2½:2½) in from beg, ending with a wrong side row.
Next row Rib 2(1:0:3), * inc in next st, rib 1, rep from * to last 4(3:0:3) sts, inc in next st, rib to end. 58(62:66:70) sts.
Change to 4 mm/No. 6 needles and cont in patt as foll:
1st row (wrong side) K1, [P1, K1] 2(3:4:5) times, work 1st row cable panel A, work 1st row cable panel B, work 1st row cable panel A, K1, [P1, K1] 2(3:4:5) times.
This row establishes the patt, placing cable panels and moss st patt edge sts. Keeping panels correct, cont inc one st at each end of every foll 6th row until there are 80(86:92:98) sts.
Cont without shaping until work measures 28(32:36:39) cm/11(12½:14:15½) in from beg, ending with a wrong side row. Cast/bind off **loosely**.

TO MAKE UP

Join shoulder seams.

NECKBAND

Using 3¼ mm/No. 4 circular needle, with right side of work facing, sl first 6(7:8:9) sts at centre front onto a safety pin, join yarn to next st, K across next 8(9:10:11) sts, [inc in next st, K1] 3 times, K up 24 sts up right side of neck, K across 32(34:38:40) sts at back neck inc 8 sts evenly, K up 24 sts down left side of neck, K across rem sts at front neck inc 3 sts evenly, turn and cast on 8 sts for underwrap. 122(126:132:136) sts.
Work in rows of K1, P1 rib.
Work 3 rows. Dec one st at each end of next 3 rows.
Next row Cast/bind off 3 sts, rib to last 2 sts, work 2 tog.
Rep last row 3 times more.
Next row Cast on 3 sts, rib to last st, inc in last st.
Rep last row 3 times more.
Inc one st at each end of next 3 rows. Work 3 rows.
Cast/bind off **loosely** in rib.
Fold neckband in half onto wrong side and catch down, lapping right side of neck over left at centre front. Set in sleeves, placing centre of cast/bound off edge to shoulder seams. Join side and sleeve seams.

see page 27

JAZZY JUMPER

Sizes

Chest	61(66:71:76) cm	24(26:28:30) in
Length	38(43:48:53) cm	15(17:19:21) in
Sleeve Seam	27(32:37:39) cm	10½(12½:14½:15½) in

Materials

3(4:5:6) 50 g/2 oz balls of *Robin Landscape DK* in main colour A.
1(1:2:2) balls in contrast colour B.
1 ball each in contrast colours C and D.
One pair each 3¼ mm/No. 4 and 4 mm/No. 6 knitting needles.
3¼ mm/No. 4 and 4 mm/No. 6 circular needles.
1 button.

Tension/gauge 24 sts and 32 rows to 10 cm/4 in over patt on 4 mm/No. 6 needles.
22 sts and 48 rows to 10 cm/4 in over g st on 3¼ mm/No. 4 needles.

Abbreviations Alt-alternate; approx-approximately; beg-beginning; cont-continu(e)(ing); cm-centimetre(s); dec-decreas(e)(ing); foll-follow(s)(ing); g-gramme(s); g st-garter stitch; in-inch(es); inc-increas(e)(ing); K-knit; mm-millimetre(s); No.-number; oz-ounce(s); P-purl; patt-pattern; rem-remain(s)(ing); rep-repeat(ing); st(s)-stitch(es).

BACK

** Using 3¼ mm/No. 4 needles and A, cast on 72(78:84:90) sts. Cont in K1, P1 rib until work measures 5 cm/2 in from beg, ending with a right side row.
Next row Rib 8(6:9:12), * inc in next st, rib 4(5:5:5), rep from * to last 9(6:9:12) sts, inc in next st, rib to end. 84(90:96:102) sts.
Change to 4 mm/No. 6 needles and cont in patt as foll:
1st row (right side) Using A, K.
2nd row Using A, K.
3rd row K3(2:3:2) A, * 2D, 2A, rep from * ending last rep 3(2:3:2) A.
4th row P3(2:3:2) A, * 2D, 2A, rep from * ending last rep 3(2:3:2) A.
5th–6th rows Rep 1st–2nd rows.
7th–8th rows Rep 3rd–4th rows using B instead of D.
9th–10th rows Rep 1st–2nd rows.
11th–12th rows Rep 3rd–4th rows using C instead of D.
13th–14th rows Rep 1st–2nd rows.
15th–16th rows Rep 3rd–4th rows using B instead of D.
These 16 rows form the patt. Cont in patt until work measures approx 23(28:33:36) cm/9(11:13:14) in from beg, ending with a 2nd, 6th, 10th or 14th patt row.
Change to 3¼ mm/No. 4 needles and cont in g st in the foll stripe sequence:
K 2 rows C, K 2 rows A, K 2 rows B, K2 rows A, K 2 rows D, K 2 rows A, K 2 rows B, K 2 rows A.
These 16 rows form the stripe sequence. ** Cont until work measures 38(43:48:53) cm/15(17:19:21) in from beg, ending with a wrong side row.

Shape Shoulders

Cast/bind off 28(30:32:34) sts, K28(30:32:34) sts including st used to cast/bind off, cast/bind off rem sts.
Leave these sts on a spare needle.

FRONT

Work as given for Back from ** to **.
Cont until work measures 28(33:37:41) cm/11(13:14½:16¼) in from beg, ending with a wrong side row.

Divide for Neck Opening

Next row K42(45:48:51), turn, leaving rem sts on a spare needle.
Complete left side of neck first.
Next row Cast on 3(3:5:5), K to end. 45(48:53:56) sts.
Cont in stripe sequence and g st until work measures

2·5 cm/1 in from beg of neck opening, ending at neck edge.
Next row K3, cast/bind off 2, K to end.
Next row K to end, casting on 2 sts over those cast/bound off in previous row.
Now cont until work measures 5 cm/2 in from beg of neck opening, ending at front edge.

Shape Neck

Cast/bind off 3(3:5:5) sts at beg of next row, 3 sts at beg of foll 4(3:4:3) alt rows then cast/bind off 2 sts at beg of every foll alt row until 28(30:32:34) sts rem.
Now cont without shaping until work measures same as Back to shoulder, ending at armhole edge.

Shape Shoulder

Cast/bind off rem sts.
With right side of work facing, return to sts on spare needle. Rejoin yarn at neck edge, cast on 3(3:5:5) sts, K to end.
Complete to match left side of neck, omitting buttonhole.

SLEEVES

Using 3¼ mm/No. 4 needles and A, cast on 38(40:42:44) sts. Cont in K1, P1 rib until work measures 5.5 cm/2¼ in from beg, ending with a right side row.
Next row Rib 6(7:8:9), * inc in next st, rib 1, rep from * to last 6(7:8:9) sts, inc in next st, rib to end. 52(54:56:58) sts.
Change to 4 mm/No. 6 needles and commence patt.
1st row (right side) Using A, K.
2nd row Using A, K.
3rd row K1(2:3:4) A, * 2D, 2A, rep from * ending last rep 1(2:3:4) A.
4th row P1(2:3:4) A, * 2D, 2A, rep from * ending last rep 1(2:3:4) A.
These 4 rows establish the patt as given on back. Cont in patt inc one st at each end of next and every foll 4th(4th:4th:3rd) row until there are 72(84:96:108) sts.
Cont without shaping until work measures approx 27(32:37:39) cm/10½(12½:14½:15½) in ending with a 2nd, 6th, 10th or 14th patt row.
Cast/bind off **loosely**.

TO MAKE UP

Join shoulder seams. Catch left front over right at base of neck opening. Use coloured threads to mark 3rd(3rd:5th:5th) st from front edge at neck.

COLLAR

Using 3¼ mm/No. 4 circular needle and A, beg at coloured thread, K up 21(21:25:29) sts up right side of neck, K across 28(30:32:34) sts on back neck, K up 21(21:25:29) sts down left side of neck to coloured thread. 70(72:82:92) sts.
Cont in rows of K1, P1 rib. Work 4 rows.
Change to 4 mm/No. 6 circular needle and cont until collar measures 6(8:9:11) cm/2½(3:3½:4½) in from beg.
Cast/bind off **loosely** in rib.
Set in sleeves, placing centre of cast/bound off edge to shoulder seams. Join side and sleeve seams. Sew on button.

see page 28

TYROLEAN TOUCH

Sizes

Chest	61(66:71) cm	24(26:28) in
Length	40(44:47) cm	16(17½:18½) in
Sleeve Seam	27(31:33) cm	10½(12¼:13) in

Materials

5(5:6) 50 g/2 oz balls of *Wendy Family Choice DK* in main colour A.
1(1:1:1) ball each in contrast colours B and C for embroidery.
One pair each 3¼ mm/No. 4 and 4 mm/No. 6 knitting needles.
Cable needle.
7(8:8) buttons.

Tension/gauge 22 sts and 30 rows to 10 cm/4 in over st st on 4 mm/No. 6 needles.

Abbreviations Alt-alternate; beg-beginning; C6F-sl next 3 sts onto cable needle and hold at front of work, K3 then K3 from cable needle; cm-centimetre(s); cont-continu(e)(ing); dec-decrease(e)(ing); foll-follow(s)(ing); g-gramme(s); in-inch(es); inc-increas(e)(ing); K-knit; mm-millimetre(s); MB-make bobble, [K1, P1, K1, P1] all into next st, turn K4, turn P4, turn [K2 tog] twice, turn K2 tog; No.-number; P-purl; patt-pattern; rep-repeat(ing); rem-remain(s)(ing); rev st st-reverse stocking stitch/stockinette stitch; st(s)-stitch(es); sl-slip; tog-together; TW2R-sl next st onto cable needle and hold at back of work, K1, then P1 from cable needle; TW2L-sl next st onto cable needle and hold at front of work, P1, then K1 from cable needle.

PANEL PATT A (worked over 6 sts)

1st row (right side) K6.
2nd row P6.
3rd–4th rows Rep 1st–2nd rows.
5th row C6F.
6th row P6.
These 6 rows form panel patt A.

PANEL PATT B (worked over 15 sts)

1st row (right side) P7, K1, P7.
2nd row K7, P1, K7.
3rd–6th rows Rep 1st–2nd rows twice.
7th row P5, TW2R, K1, TW2L, P5.
8th and 4 foll alt rows K the P sts and P the K sts of previous row.
9th row P4, TW2R, P1, K1, P1, TW2L, P4.
11th row P3, TW2R, P2, K1, P2, TW2L, P3.
13th row P2, TW2R, P3, K1, P3, TW2L, P2.
15th row P1, TW2R, P4, K1, P4, TW2L, P1.
17th row P1, MB, P5, MB, P5, MB, P1.
18th row K.
19th row P.
20th row K.
21st–24th rows Rep 19th–20th rows twice.
These 24 rows form panel patt B.

BACK

Using 3¼ mm/No. 4 needles and A, cast on 64(70:74) sts.
Cont in K1, P1 rib for 5(5:6) cm/2(2:2½) in, ending with a right side row.
Next row Rib 12(5:7), * inc in next st, rib 1(2:2), rep from * to last 12(5:7) sts, inc in next st, rib to end. 85(91:95) sts.
Change to 4 mm/No. 6 needles and cont in patt as foll:
1st row (right side) P7(8:8), work 1st row panel patt A, P2(4:6), * work 1st row panel patt A, work 1st row panel patt B, work 1st row panel patt A *, P1, work from * to * again, P2(4:6), work 1st row panel patt A, P7(8:8).
2nd row K7(8:8), work 2nd row panel patt A, K2(4:6), * work 2nd row panel patt A, work 2nd row panel patt B, work 2nd row panel patt B *, K1, rep from * to * again, K2(4:6), work 2nd row panel patt A, K7(8:8).
These 2 rows establish the patt, placing panel patts and

edge sts in rev st st. Keeping panel patts correct, cont until work measures 26(29:31) cm/10(11½:12¼) in from beg, ending with a wrong side row.
Shape Armholes
Cast/bind off 4(5:5) sts at beg of next 2 rows. Dec one st at each end of every row until 65(71:75) sts rem.
Cont without shaping until work measures 40(44:47) cm/16(17½:18½) in from beg, ending with a wrong side row.
Shape Shoulders
Cast/bind off 8(9:10) sts at beg of next 2 rows and 9(10:10) sts at beg of foll 2 rows. Leave rem 31(33:35) sts on a spare needle.

LEFT FRONT

Using 3¼ mm/No. 4 needles and A, cast on 32(35:37) sts.
Cont in K1, P1 rib as foll:
1st row (right side) K0(1:1), * P1, K1, rep from * to end.
2nd row * P1, K1, rep from * to last 0(1:1) sts, P0(1:1).
Rep these 2 rows until work measures 5(5:6) cm/2(2:2½) in from beg, ending with a right side row.
Next row Rib 1(2:3), * inc in next st, rib 2, rep from * to last 1(3:4) sts, inc in next st, rib 0(2:3). 43(46:48) sts.
Change to 4 mm/No. 6 needles and cont in patt as foll:
1st row (right side) P7(8:8), work 1st row panel patt A, P2(4:6), work 1st row panel patt A, work 1st row panel patt B, work 1st row panel patt A, P1.
2nd row K1, work 2nd row panel patt A, work 2nd row panel patt B, work 2nd row panel patt A, K2(4:6), work 2nd row panel patt A, K7(8:8).
These 2 rows establish the patt, placing panel patts and edge sts in rev st st. Cont in patt, keeping panel patts correct, until work measures same as Back to armhole, ending with a wrong side row.
Shape Armhole
Cast/bind off 4(5:5) sts at beg of next row. Work 1 row.
Dec one st at armhole edge on every row until 30(32:34) sts rem.
Cont without shaping until work measures 36(39:42) cm/14(15½:16½) in from beg, ending with a wrong side row.
Shape Neck
Next row Patt to last 6(7:7) sts, turn leaving these sts on a safety pin.
Dec one st at neck edge on every row until until 17(19:20) sts rem.
Cont without shaping until work measures same as Back to shoulder, ending with a wrong side row.
Shape Shoulder
Cast/bind off 8(9:10) sts at beg of next row. Work 1 row. Cast/bind off rem 9(10:10) sts.

RIGHT FRONT

Work to match left front, reversing placing of panel patts and all shapings.

SLEEVES

Using 3¼ mm/No. 4 needles and A, cast on 36(38:40) sts.
Cont in K1, P1 rib until work measures 4(5:5) cm/1½(2:2) in from beg, ending with a right side row.
Next row Rib 3(4:5), * inc in next st, rib 1, rep from * to last 3(4:5) sts, rib to end. 51(53:55) sts.
Change to 4 mm/No. 6 needles and cont in patt as foll:
1st row (right side) P4(5:6), work 1st row panel patt B, work 1st row panel patt A, P1, work 1st row panel patt A, work 1st row panel patt B, P4(5:6).
2nd row K4(5:6), work 2nd row panel patt B, work 2nd row panel patt A, K1, work 2nd row panel patt A, work 2nd row panel patt B, K4(5:6).
These 2 rows establish the patt, placing the panel patts and edge sts in rev st st. Keeping panel patts correct, cont inc and work into rev st st one st at each end of 5th and every foll 7th(6th:6th) row until there are 67(73:77) sts.
Cont without shaping until work measures 27(31:33) cm/10½(12¼:13) in from beg, ending with a wrong side row.
Shape Top/Cap
Cast/bind off 4(5:5) sts at beg of next 2 rows. Dec one st at each end of next and every foll alt row until 29 sts rem, ending with a wrong side row. Cast/bind off.

TO MAKE UP
Join shoulder seams.

NECKBAND
With right side of work facing, using 3¼ mm/No. 4 needles and A, K across 6(7:7) sts on right front safety pin, K up 14(15:16) sts up right side of neck, K across 31(33:35) sts at back neck, K up 14(15:16) sts down left side of neck then K across 6(7:7) sts on left front safety pin. 71(77:81) sts.

Beg with a wrong side row, cont in K1, P1 rib as given for 2nd size of left front until neckband measures 3 cm/1¼ in from beg, ending with a wrong side row. Cast/bind off **loosely** in rib.

BUTTONBAND
With right side of work facing, using 3¼ mm/No. 4 needles and A, K up 109(117:125) sts evenly down left front and neckband.

Beg with a wrong side row, cont in K1, P1 rib as given for neckband until buttonband measures 3 cm/1¼ in from beg. Cast/bind off in rib.

BUTTONHOLE BAND
With right side of work facing, using 3¼ mm/No. 4 needles and A, K up 109(117:125) sts evenly up right front and neckband.

Beg with a wrong side row work 3 rows K1, P1 rib as given for neckband.

Next row Rib 6(5:5), * cast/bind off 2 sts, rib 14(13:14) including st used to cast/bind off, rep from * ending last rep rib 5(5:6).

Next row Rib to end, casting on 2 sts over those cast/bound off in previous row.

Cont in rib until band measures 3 cm/1¼ in from beg. Cast/bind off in rib.

Embroider leaves and flowers as shown in photograph. Join side and sleeve seams. Set in sleeves gathering at shoulder. Sew on buttons.

---

see page 29

JOLLY HOCKEY STICKS

Sizes

Chest	61(66:71:77) cm	24(26:28:30) in
Length	44(48:51:55) cm	17½(19:20:21¾) in
Sleeve Seam	31(35:39:43) cm	12¼(13¾:15½:17) in

Materials
3(3:4:4) 50 g/2 oz balls of *Lister Richmond DK* in main colour A.
2(2:2:2) balls in contrast colour B.
1(1:1:1) ball in contrast colour C.
One pair each 3¼ mm/No. 4 and 4 mm/No. 6 knitting needles.

Tension/gauge 26 sts and 26 rows to 10 cm/4 in over patt on 4 mm/No. 6 needles.

Abbreviations Beg-beginning; cm-centimetre(s); cont-continu(e)(ing); dec-decreas(e)(ing); foll-follow(s)(ing); g-gramme(s); in-inch(es); inc- increas(e)(ing); K-knit; mm-millimetre(s); No.-number; oz-ounce(s); P-purl; patt-pattern; rem-remain(s)(ing); rep-repeat(ing); st(s)-stitch(es); st st-stocking stitch/stockinette stitch; sl-slip.

BACK
** Using 3¼ mm/No. 4 needles and A, cast on 68 (74:80:86) sts. Cont in K2, P2 rib as foll:
1st row (right side) K0(2:0:2), * P2, K2 rep from * to end.
2nd row * P2, K2, rep from * to last 0(2:0:2) sts, P0(2:0:2).
Rep these 2 rows until work measures 7(7:8:8) cm/2¾(2¾:3:3) in from beg, ending with a right side row.
Next row Rib 4(7:7:10), * inc in next st, rib 2, rep from * to last 4(7:7:10) sts, inc in next st, rib to end. 89(95:103:109) sts.
Change to 4 mm/No. 6 needles. Beg with a K row cont in st st working colour patt from chart. Read K rows from right to left and P rows from left to right. **
Cont until work measures 44(48:51:55) cm/17½ (19:20:21¾) in from beg, ending with a P row.
Shape Shoulders
Cast/bind off 15(16:18:19) sts at beg of next 4 rows.
Leave rem 29(31:31:33) sts on a spare needle.

FRONT
Work as given for Back from ** to **.
Cont until work measures 39(43:46:50) cm/15½ 17:18:19½) in from beg, ending with a P row.
Shape Neck
Next row Patt 39(41:45:47) sts and turn leaving rem sts on a spare needle.
Complete left side of neck first.
Dec one st at neck edge on every row until 30(32:36:38) sts rem.

Cont without shaping until work measures same as Back to shoulder, ending at armhole edge.
Shape Shoulder
Cast/bind off 15(16:18:19) sts at beg of next row. Work 1 row. Cast/bind off rem 15(16:18:19) sts.
With right side of work facing return to sts on spare needle. Sl centre 11(13:13:15) sts onto a stitch holder, rejoin yarn at neck edge, patt to end.
Complete to match first side of neck.

SLEEVES
Using 3¼ mm/No. 4 needles and A, cast on 42(42:44:46) sts. Cont. in K2, P2 rib as given for 2nd(2nd:1st:2nd) size of Back until work measures 4(4:5:5) cm/1½ (1½:2:2) in from beg, ending with a right side row.
Next row Rib 3(1:2:3), * inc in next st, rib 1, rep from * to last 3(1:2:3) sts, inc in next st, rib to end. 61(63:65:67) sts.
Change to 4 mm/No. 6 needles. Beg with a K row cont in st st working colour patt from chart, **at the same time**, inc one st at each end of 3rd and every foll 5th (5th:4th:4th) row until there are 85(91:101:111) sts.
Cont without shaping until work measures 31 (35:39:43) cm/12¼(13¾:15½:17) in from beg, ending with a P row. Cast/bind off **loosely**.

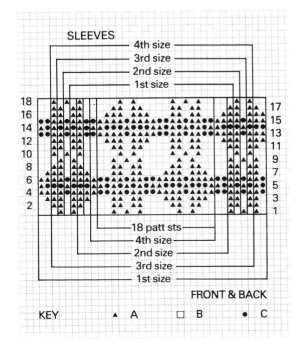

SLEEVES
4th size
3rd size
2nd size
1st size
18 16 14 12 10 8 6 4 2
17 15 13 11 9 7 5 3 1
18 patt sts
4th size
2nd size
3rd size
1st size
FRONT & BACK

KEY ▲ A ☐ B ● C

TO MAKE UP
Join right shoulder seam.

POLO COLLAR
With right side of work facing, using 3¼ mm/No. 4 needles and A, K up 22(23:24:25) sts down left side of neck, K across 11(13:13:15) sts at centre front inc 3 sts evenly, K up 22(23:24:25) sts up right side of neck, then K across 29(31:31:33) sts at back neck inc 5 sts evenly. 92 (98:100:106) sts.

Cont in K2, P2 rib as given for Back until collar measures 8(10:11:12) cm/3(4:4½:4¾) in from beg. Cast/bind off **loosely** in rib.

Join left shoulder and neckband, reversing seam on collar for last 4 cm/1¾ in. Set in sleeves, placing centre of cast/ bound off edge to shoulder seam. Join side and sleeve seams.

see page 30

WINSOME WAISTCOAT

Sizes
Chest	61(66:71:76) cm	24(26:28:30) in
Length	43(48:53:57) cm	17(19:21:22½) in

Materials
5(6:6:6) 50 g/2 oz balls of *Twilleys Perlespun* 4 ply.
One pair each 2¾ mm/No. 2 and 3¼ mm/No. 4 knitting needles.
5 buttons.

Tension/gauge 27 sts and 39 rows to 10 cm/4 in over patt on 3¼ mm/No. 4 needles.

Abbreviations Alt-alternate; beg-beginning; cm- centimetre(s); cont-continu(e)(ing); dec-decreas(e) (ing); foll-follow(s)(ing); g-gramme(s); in-inch(es); inc-increas(e)(ing); K-knit; mm-millimetre(s); No.- number; oz-ounce(s); P-purl; patt-pattern; rem-re- main(s)(ing); rep-repeat(ing); rev st st-reverse stocking/stockinette stitch; st(s)-stitch(es); st st- stocking/stockinette stitch.

BACK
Using 2¾ mm/No. 2 needles, cast on 74(82:86:94) sts.
Cont in K2, P2 rib as foll:
1st row (right side) K2, * P2, K2, rep from * to end.
2nd row P2, * K2, P2, rep from * to end.
Rep the last 2 rows for 6 cm/2½ in, ending with a right side row.
Next row Rib 6(12:10:17) * inc in next st, rib 1, rep from * to last 8(14:12:17) sts, inc in next st, rib to end. 105(111:119:125) sts.

Change to 3¼ mm/No. 4 needles and commence patt from chart. Read right side rows from right to left and wrong side rows from left to right.
1st row (right side) K3(6:3:6), P0(0:1:1), K0(0:6:6), * K7, P1, K6, rep from * to last 4(7:11:14) sts, K4(7:7:7), P0(0:1:1), K0(0:3:6).
2nd row P4(0:2:5), K0(1:3:3), P0(6:6:6), * P5, K3, P6, rep from * to last 3(6:10:13) sts, P3(5:5:5), K0(1:3:3), P0(0:2:5).
Cont in patt from chart until work measures 43(48:53:57) cm/17(19:21:22½) in from beg, ending with a wrong side row.

Shape Shoulders
Cast/bind off 16(17:18:19) sts at beg of next 4 rows.
Leave rem 41(43:47:49) sts on a spare needle.

LEFT FRONT
Using 2¾ mm/No. 2 needles, cast on 34(38:42:46) sts.
Cont in K2, P2 rib as for Back until work measures 6 cm/2½ in from beg, ending with a right side row.
Next row Rib 1(4:6:3), * inc in next st, rib 1(1:1:2), rep from * to last 3(6:8:4) sts, inc in next st, rib to end. 50(53:57:60) sts.
Change to 3¼ mm/No. 4 needles and cont in patt from chart until work measures 23 rows less than Back to shoulder, ending at front edge.

Shape Neck
Cast/bind off 10 sts at beg of next row. Dec one st at neck edge on next 2 rows, then on every foll alt row until 32(34:36:38) sts rem.
Cont without shaping, work 8(6:2:0) rows, ending at armhole edge.

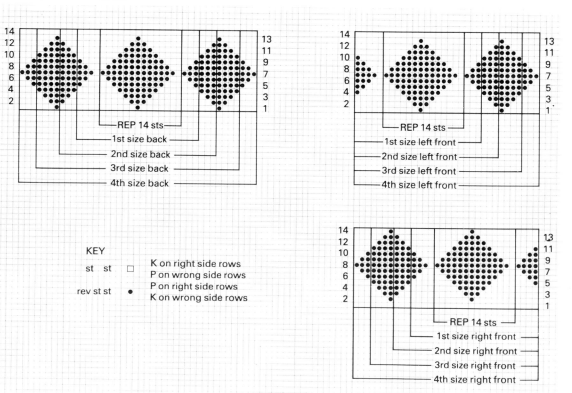

KEY

st st	□	K on right side rows P on wrong side rows
rev st st	●	P on right side rows K on wrong side rows

Shape Shoulder
Cast/bind off 16(17:18:19) sts at beg of next row. Work 1 row. Cast/bind off rem sts.

RIGHT FRONT
Work as for left front, foll appropriate chart for patt and reversing shapings.

TO MAKE UP
Join shoulder seams. Mark the position of armholes 20(22:24:26) cm/8(8½:9½:10¼) in down from shoulder seams.

NECKBAND
Using 2¾ mm/No. 2 needles and with right side of work facing, K up 28(29:29:30) sts up right front neck, K across 41(43:47:49) sts on back neck, K up 29(30:30:31) sts down left front neck. 98(102:106:110) sts.
Beg with a 2nd row cont in K2, P2 rib as for Back. Work 9 rows. Cast/bind off **loosely** in rib.

BUTTONHOLE BAND
Using 2¾ mm/No. 2 needles and with right side of work facing, K up 134(150:166:182) sts up right front edge.
Beg with a 2nd row cont in K2, P2 rib as for Back. Work 3 rows.
1st buttonhole row Rib 4, [cast off 2 sts, rib 29(33:37:41)] 4 times, cast off 2 sts, rib 4.
2nd buttonhole row Rib to end, casting on 2 sts over those cast off in previous row.
Work 4 rows. Cast/bind off in rib.

BUTTONBAND
Work to match buttonhole band omitting buttonholes.

ARMBANDS
Using 2¾ mm/No. 2 needles and with right side of work facing, K up 142(158:174:190) sts evenly around armhole edge between markers. Beg with a 2nd row cont in K2, P2 rib as for Back. Work 9 rows. Cast/bind off in rib.
Join side seams. Sew on buttons.

---

see page 31

CASTAWAY

Sizes
Chest	61(66:71:76) cm	24(26:28:30) in
Length	42(44:46:48) cm	16½(17½:18:19) in
Sleeve Seam	34(36:37·5:39·5) cm	13½(14:14¾:15¾) in

Materials
7(8:9:10) 50 g/2 oz balls of *Pingouin Fil d'Ecosse* 3
One pair each 3¼ mm/No. 4 and 4 mm/No. 6 knitting needles.
Cable needle.

Tension/gauge 21 sts and 26 rows to 10 cm/4 in over rev st st on 4 mm/No. 6 needles.

Abbreviations Alt-alternate; beg-beginning; cm-centimetre(s); cont-continu(e)(ing); C4F-sl next 2 sts onto cable needle and hold at front of work, K2 then K2 from cable needle; C4B-sl next 2 sts onto cable needle and hold at back of work, K2 then K2 from cable needle; C5B-sl next 3 sts onto cable needle and hold at back of work, K2, sl centre st from cable needle onto left hand needle and K, K2 from cable needle; foll-follow(s)(ing); g-gramme(s); in-inch(es); inc-increase(e)(ing); K-knit; mm-millimetre(s); No.-number; oz-ounce(s); P-purl; patt-pattern; rem-remain(s)(ing); rep-repeat(ing); rev st st-reverse stocking stitch/stockinette stitch; st(s)-stitch(es); sl-slip; SCF-sl next 2 sts onto cable needle and hold at front of work, K1, then K2 from cable needle; SCB-sl next st onto cable needle and hold at back of work, K2 then K1 from cable needle; tbl-through back of loop(s).

CABLE PANEL (worked over 29 sts)
1st row (wrong side) K4, P2, K3, P2, K1, P2, [K1, P1] 5 times, K1, P2, K2.
2nd row P2, K3, [P1, K1] 5 times, C5B, P3, K2, P4.
3rd row As 1st row.
4th row P2, K3, [P1, K1] 4 times, C4B, P1, C4F, SCB, P4.
5th row K5, P4, K1, [P1 tbl, K1] twice, P2, K1, [P1, K1] 4 times, P2, K2.
6th row P2, SCF, [P1, K1] 3 times, C4B, P1, [K1 tbl, P1] twice, C4F, P5.
7th row K5, P4, K1, [P1 tbl, K1] 3 times, P2, [K1, P1] 3 times, P2, K3.
8th row P3, SCF, K1, P1, K1, C4B, P1, [K1 tbl, P1] 3 times, K4, P5.
9th row K5, P4, K1, [P1 tbl, K1] 4 times, P2, K1, P1, K1, P2, K4.
10th row P4, SCF, C4B, P1, [K1 tbl, P1] 4 times, C4F, P5.
11th row K5, P4, K1, [P1 tbl, K1] 5 times, P4, K5.
12th row P5, C4F, P1, [K1 tbl, P1] 4 times, C4B, SCF, P4.

13th row K4, P2, K1, P1, K1, P2, K1, [P1 tbl, K1] 4 times, P4, K5.
14th row P5, K4, P1, [K1 tbl, P1] 3 times, C4B, K1, P1, K1, SCF, P3.
15th row K3, P3, [K1, P1] twice, K1, P2, K1, [P1 tbl, K1] 3 times, P4, K5.
16th row P5, C4F, [P1, K1 tbl] twice, P1, C4B, [K1, P1] 3 times, SCF, P2.
17th row K2, P2, K1, [P1, K1] 4 times, P2, K1, [P1 tbl, K1] twice, P4, K5.
18th row P4, SCB, C4F, P1, C4B, K1, [P1, K1] 4 times, K2, P2.
19th row K2, P2, K1, [P1, K1] 5 times, P2, K1, P2, K3, P2, K4.
20th row P4, K2, P3, C5B, K1, [P1, K1] 5 times, K2, P2.
21st row K2, P2, K1, [P1, K1] 5 times, P2, K1, P2, K3, P2, K4.
22nd row P4, SCF, C4B, P1, C4F, K1, [P1, K1] 4 times, K2, P2.
23rd row K2, P2, K1, [P1, K1] 4 times, P2, K1, [P1 tbl, K1] twice, P4, K5.
24th row P5, C4F, P1, [K1 tbl, P1] twice, C4F, K1, [P1, K1] twice, P1, SCB, P2.
25th row K3, P2, [P1, K1] 3 times, P2, K1, [P1 tbl, K1] 3 times, P4, K5.
26th row P5, K4, P1, [K1 tbl, P1] 3 times, C4F, K1, P1, K1, SCB, P3.
27th row K4, P2, K1, P1, K1, P2, K1, [P1 tbl, K1] 4 times, P4, K5.
28th row P5, C4F, P1, [K1 tbl, P1] 4 times, C4F, SCB, P4.
29th row K5, P4, K1, [P1 tbl, K1] 5 times, P4, K5.
30th row P4, SCB, C4F, P1, [K1 tbl, P1] 4 times, C4F, P5.
31st row K5, P4, K1, [P1 tbl, K1] 4 times, P2, K1, P1, K1, P2, K4.
32nd row P3, SCB, K1, P1, K1, C4F, P1, [K1 tbl, P1] 3 times, K4, P5.
33rd row K5, P4, K1, [P1 tbl, K1] 3 times, P2, [K1, P1] 3 times, P2, K3.
34th row P2, SCB, [P1, K1] 3 times, C4F, P1, [K1 tbl, P1] twice, C4F, P5.
35th row K5, P4, K1, [P1 tbl, K1] twice, P2, K1, [P1, K1] 4 times, P2, K2.
36th row P2, K3, [P1, K1] 4 times, C4F, P1, C4B, SCF, P4.
These 36 rows form the cable panel.

BACK
** Using 3¼ mm/No. 4 needles cast on 79(83:87:91) sts.
Cont in K1, P1 rib as foll:
1st row (right side) K1, * P1, K1, rep from * to end.
2nd row P1, * K1, P1, rep from * to end.
Rep these 2 rows until work measures 6 cm/2½ in from beg, ending with a wrong side row. Inc one st at each end

of last row for 3rd and 4th sizes only. 79(83:89:93) sts.
Change to 4 mm/No. 6 needles and cont in patt as foll:
1st row (wrong side) K4(5:7:8), work 1st row cable panel, K13(15:17:19), work 1st row cable panel, K4(5:7:8).
2nd row P4(5:7:8), work 2nd row cable panel, P13(15:17:19), work 2nd row cable panel, P4(5:7:8).
These 2 rows establish the patt, placing two cable panels on a rev st st background. Keeping panels correct, cont in patt until work measures 27(28:29:30) cm/10½(11:11½:12) in from beg, ending with a wrong side row.

Shape Armholes
Cast/bind off 2(2:3:3) sts at beg of next 2 rows. 75(79:83:87) sts. **
Now cont without shaping until work measures 42(44:46:48) cm/16½(17½:18:19) in from beg, ending with a wrong side row.

Shape Shoulders
Next row Cast/bind off 21(22:23:24) sts, patt 33(35:37:39) sts including st used to cast/bind off, cast/bind off rem 21(22:23:24) sts. Leave these sts on a spare needle.

FRONT
Work as given for Back from ** to **.
Now Cont without shaping until work measures 18 rows less than Back to shoulder, ending with a wrong side row.

Shape Neck
Next row Patt 36(37:38:39) sts and turn leaving rem sts on a spare needle.
Complete left side of neck first.
Cast/bind off 4 sts at beg of next row, 3 sts at beg of foll alt row and 2 sts at beg of next 2 alt rows. Now dec one st at neck edge on 4 foll alt rows. 21(22:23:24) sts.
Cont without shaping until work matches Back to shoulder.

Shape Shoulder
Cast/bind off rem sts.
With right side of work facing return to sts on spare needle. Sl centre 3(5:7:9) sts onto a stitch holder, rejoin yarn at neck edge, patt to end.

Patt 1 row. Complete to match first side of neck.

SLEEVES
Using 3¼ mm/No. 4 needles cast on 41(43:45:47) sts.
Cont in K1, P1 rib as given on Back until work measures 6 cm/2½ in from beg, ending with a right side row.
Next row Rib 14(9:7:6), * inc in next st, rib 12(7:5:4), rep from * to last 14(10:8:6) sts, inc in next st, rib to end. 43(47:51:55) sts.
Change to 4 mm/No. 6 needles and cont in patt as foll:
1st row (wrong side) K7(9:11:13), work 1st row cable panel, K7(9:11:13).
2nd row P7(9:11:13), work 2nd row cable panel, P7(9:11:13).
These 2 rows establish the patt, placing cable panel with edge sts in rev st st. Keeping panel correct, cont inc and work into rev st st one st at each end of 5th(7th:9th:11th) row and every foll 6th row until there are 65(69:71:75) sts.
Cont without shaping until work measures 35(37:39:41) cm/13¾(14½:15½:16¼) in from beg, ending with a wrong side row. Cast/bind off **loosely**.

TO MAKE UP
Join right shoulder seam.

NECKBAND
With right side of work facing, using 3¼ mm/No. 4 needles, K up 22 sts down left side of neck, K across 3(5:7:9) sts at centre front, K up 21 sts up right side of neck, K across 33(35:37:39) sts at back neck. 79(83:87:91) sts.
Beg with a wrong side row, cont in K1, P1 rib as given for Back until neckband measures 5 cm/2 in from beg. Cast/bind off **loosely** in rib.
Join left shoulder and neckband. Fold neckband onto right side and slip stitch neatly in place.
Set in sleeves, joining final rows to cast/bound off sts at underarm.
Join side and sleeve seams.

see page 32

IN THE SWING

Sizes

Chest	61(66:71:76) cm	24(26:28:30) in
Length	43(48:53:57) cm	17(19:21:22½) in
Sleeve Seam	28(31:35:38) cm	11(12¼:13¾:15) in

Materials
8(9:9:10) 50 g/2 oz balls of *Twilleys Stalite No. 3*.
One pair each 3 mm/No. 3 and 3¾ mm/No. 5 knitting needles.

Tension/gauge 27 sts and 46 rows to 10 cm/4 in over patt on 3¾ mm/No. 5 needles.

Abbreviations Alt-alternate; beg-beginning; cont-continu(e)(ing); cm-centimetre(s); dec-decreas(e)(ing); foll-follow(s)(ing); g-gramme(s); in-inch(es); inc-increas(e)(ing); K-knit; No.-number; oz-ounce(s); P-purl; patt-pattern; rem-remain(s)(ing); rep-repeat(ing); st(s)-stitch(es); sl-slip; ybk-yarn back; ytf-yarn to front.

FRONT
** Using 3 mm/No. 3 needles, cast on 83(87:91:95) sts.
Cont in K1, P1 rib as foll:
1st row (right side) K1, * P1, K1, rep from * to end.
2nd row P1, * K1, P1, rep from * to end.
Rep these 2 rows until work measures 5 cm/2 in from beg, ending with a wrong side row.
Next row Rib 4(9:11:13), * inc in next st, rib 2, rep from * to last 4(9:11:13) sts, inc in next st, rib to end. 109(111:115:119) sts.
Change to 3¾ mm/No. 5 needles.
Next row P.

Now cont in patt as foll:
1st row (right side) K1, [ytf sl 1, P1] 0(0:1:2) times, [ybk sl 1, P1] 0(1:1:1) times, P1, [ybk sl 1, P2] 3 times, ybk sl 1, * [P1, ytf sl 1] 5 times, P1, [ybk sl 1, P2] 4 times, ybk sl 1, rep from * to last 1(3:5) sts, [P1, ytf sl 1] 0(0:1:2) times, K1.
2nd row K1, [K1, ybk sl 1] 0(0:1:2) times, [P1, K2] 4 times, * P1, [ybk sl 1, K1] 5 times, ybk sl 1, [P1, K2] 4 times, rep from * to last 0(2:4:6) sts, P0(1:1:1), [ybk sl 1, K1] 0(0:1:2) times, K0(1:1:1).
3rd–11th rows Rep 1st–2nd rows 4 times more, then work 1st row again.
12th row P.
13th row K1, P0(0:0:1), [ybk sl 1] 0(0:0:1) times, P0(0:2:2), [ybk sl 1] 0(1:1:1) times, P0(1:1:1), [ytf sl 1, P1] 5 times, ybk sl 1, * [P2, ybk sl 1] 4 times, [P1, ytf sl 1] 5 times, P1, ybk sl 1, rep from * to last 1(3:5) sts, P0(0:2:2), [ybk sl 1] 0(0:0:1) times, P0(0:0:1), K1.
14th row K1, K0(0:0:1), P0(0:0:1), K0(0:2:2), P1, * ybk sl 1, [K1, ybk sl 1] 5 times, [P1, K2] 4 times, P1, rep from * to last 11(13:15:17) sts, [ybk sl 1, K1] 5 times, [ybk sl 1] 0(1:1:1) times, P0(1:1:1), K0(0:2:2), P0(0:0:1), K1(1:1:2).
15th–23rd rows Rep 13th–14th rows 4 times more, then work 13th row again.
24th row P.
These 24 rows form the patt. ** Cont in patt until work measures 30(34:38:41) cm/12(13½:15:16) in from beg, ending with a wrong side row.

Shape Neck
Next row Patt 54(55:57:59) sts and turn leaving rem sts on a spare needle.
Complete left side of neck first.

Dec one st at neck edge on next and every foll 3rd row until 34(34:35:36) sts rem.
Cont without shaping, work 1(2:5:6) rows, ending at armhole edge.

Shape Shoulder
Cast/bind off 17(17:17:18) sts at beg of next row. Work 1 row. Cast/bind off rem 17(17:18:18) sts.
With right side of work facing, return to sts on spare needle. Sl centre st onto a safety pin, rejoin yarn to neck edge, patt to end.
Work 1 row.
Complete to match first side of neck.

BACK
Work as given for Front from ** to **.
Cont in patt until work measures same as Front to shoulder, ending with a wrong side row.

Shape Shoulders
Cast/bind off 17(17:17:18) sts at beg of next 2 rows and 17(17:18:18) sts at beg of next 2 rows. 41(43:45:47) sts.
Change to 3 mm/No. 3 needles. Cont in K1, P1 rib as given for Front. Work 4 rows. Cast/bind off in rib.

SLEEVES
Using 3 mm/No. 3 needles, cast on 39(43:47:51) sts.
Cont in K1, P1 rib as given for Front until work measures 5 cm/2 in from beg, ending with a wrong side row.
Next row Rib 9(2:4:6), * inc in next st, rib 0(1:1:1), rep from * to last 9(3:5:7) sts, inc in next st, rib to end. 61(63:67:71) sts.
Change to 3¾ mm/No. 5 needles.
Next row P.
Now cont in patt as given for Front, inc one st at each end of the 5th and every foll 8th row until there are

83(87:91:95) sts.
Cont without shaping until work measures 28(31:35:38) cm/11(12¼:13¾:15) in from beg, ending with a wrong side row. Cast/bind off **loosely**.

NECK INSET
Using 3 mm/No. 3 needles, with right side of work facing, K up st from safety pin at centre front.
1st row (P1, K1, P1) all into st.
2nd row K1, P1, K1.
3rd row Inc in first st, K1, inc in last st.
4th row [P1, K1] twice, P1.
5th row Inc in first st, P1, K1, P1, inc in last st.
6th row [K1, P1] 3 times, K1.
Cont as set in K1, P1 rib, inc one st at each end of next and every foll alt row until there are 51(55:59:63) sts, ending with a wrong side row.
Shape Neck
Next 2 rows Rib 12, turn and rib to end.
Next 2 rows Rib 10, turn and rib to end.
Next 2 rows Rib 8, turn and rib to end.
Cast/bind off these 8 sts.
Sl 4 sts down left side of neck and 27(31:35:39) sts at centre front onto a stitch holder. With right side of work facing rejoin yarn to rem 12 sts, rib to end.
Complete to match first side of neck, reversing shaping.
Sl 4 sts down right side of neck onto stitch holder.
Cast/bind off 31(35:39:43) sts on holder, in rib.

TO MAKE UP
Join shoulder seams. Sew sides of neck inset in place and to sides of back neckband. Set in sleeves, placing centre of cast/bound off edge to shoulder seams. Join side and sleeve seams.

---

see page 34

ALPHA BETA

Sizes

Chest	61(66:71:76) cm	24(26:28:30) in
Length	38(43:47:53) cm	15(17:18½:21) in
Sleeve Seam	30(34:38:42) cm	12(13½:15:16½) in

Materials
5(6:7:8) 50 g/2 oz balls of *Scheepjeswol Mayflower Cotton Helarsgarn* in main colour A.
1(1:1:1) ball each in contrast colours B, C, D and E.
One pair each 3¼ mm/No. 4 and 4 mm/No. 6 knitting needles.
4(5:5:6) buttons.

Tension/gauge 20 sts and 22 rows to 10 cm/4 in over st st on 4 mm/No. 6 needles.

> **Abbreviations** Alt-alternate; beg-beginning; cm-centimetre(s); cont-continu(e)(ing); dec-decreas(e)(ing); foll-follow(s)(ing); g-gramme(s); g st-garter stitch; in-inch(es); inc-increas(e)(ing); K-knit; mm-millimetre(s); No.-number; oz-ounce(s); P-purl; patt-pattern; rem-remain(s)(ing); rep-repeat(ing); st(s)-stitch(es); st st-stocking stitch/stockinette stitch.

BACK
Using 3¼ mm/No. 4 needles and A, cast on 58(64:70:76) sts. Cont in K1, P1 rib. Work 11(13:13:15) rows, ending with a right side row.
Next row Rib 9(9:10:13), * inc in next st, rib 7(8:9:9), rep from * to last 9(10:10:13) sts, inc in next st, rib to end. 64(70:76:82) sts. Change to 4 mm/No. 6 needles. Beg with a K row cont in st st working colour patt from chart. Read K rows from right to left and P rows from left to right. Strand yarn not in use loosely across back of work, twist yarns when changing colour to avoid a hole.
Cont until 72(84:92:104) rows have been worked from chart, ending with a P row.
Shape Shoulders

Cast/bind off 22(24:26:28) sts at beg of next 2 rows. Cast/bind off rem 20(22:24:26) sts.

LEFT FRONT
** Using 3¼ mm/No. 4 needles and A, cast on 29(32:35:38) sts. Cont in K1, P1 rib as foll:
1st row (right side) K1(0:1:0), * P1, K1, rep from * to end.
2nd row * P1, K1, rep from * to last 1(0:1:0) sts, P1(0:1:0).
Rep these 2 rows 4(5:5:6) times more, then work 1st row again.
Next row Rib 7(8:9:10), * inc in next st, rib 6(7:7:8), rep from * to last 8(8:10:10) sts, inc in next st, rib to end. 32(35:38:41) sts.
Change to 4 mm/No. 6 needles. Beg with a K row cont in st st and colour patt from chart. **
Cont until 47(59:67:73) rows have been worked, ending with a K row.
Shape Neck
Dec one st at beg of next and every foll alt row until 22(24:26:28) sts rem.
Cont without shaping until work measures same as Back to shoulder, ending at armhole edge.
Shape Shoulder
Cast off rem sts.

RIGHT FRONT
Work as given for left front from ** to **.
Cont until 46(58:66:72) rows have been worked, ending with a P row.
Complete to match left front.

SLEEVES
Using 3¼ mm/No. 4 needles and A, cast on 34 sts. Cont in K1, P1 rib, work 13(15:15:17) rows, ending with a right side row.
Next row Rib 1, * inc in next st, rib 1, rep from * to last st, rib 1. 50 sts.
Change to 4 mm/No. 6 needles. Beg with a K row cont in

st st and work colour patt from chart, **at the same time**, inc one st at each end of every foll 3rd row until there are 80(86:90:96) sts.

Cont without shaping until work measures 30(34:38:42) cm/12(13½:15:16½) in from beg, ending with a P row.

Cast/bind off **loosely**.

UNDERARM INSERTS (make 2)

Using 3¼ mm/No. 4 needles and A, cast on one st.

Next row K into front, back and front of st. 3 sts.

Next row Inc in first st, K1, inc in last st.

Cont in g st and stripe sequence of 2 rows B, 2 rows A, **at the same time**, inc one st at each end of every foll alt row until there are 17(19:19:21) sts.

Now dec one st at each end of every alt row until one st rem.

Fasten off.

TO MAKE UP

Join shoulder seams. Place coloured markers 1 cm/½ in below neck shaping on each Front.

COLLAR (left side)

Using 3¼ mm/No. 4 needles and A, cast on 6(6:7:8) sts.

Work 4 rows g st. Cont in g st in stripes of 2 rows B, 2 rows A until band is long enough, when slightly stretched, to fit up right front to coloured marker.

Inc one st at inner neck edge on every row until there are 18(20:22:24) sts.

Cont without shaping until collar fits round to centre back neck.

Cast/bind off.

COLLAR (right side)

Sew left side of collar and band in place. Mark the position of 4(5:5:6) buttons on band, the first 1 cm/½ in above cast on edge, the last 2 rows below coloured marker, with the others evenly spaced between.

Work right side of collar to match left side, making buttonholes opposite markers for buttons as foll:

1st row (right side) K2(2:2:3), cast/bind off 2 sts, K to end.

2nd row K to end, casting on 2 sts over those cast/bound off in previous row.

Sew right side of collar and band in place, joining centre back.

Set in sleeves placing centre of cast/bound off edge to shoulder seams.

Sew underarm inserts in place. Join rem side and sleeve seams. Sew on buttons.

KEY
□ A
■ B
× C
▲ D
● E

see page 35

CASUAL COVER-UP

Sizes

Chest	61(66:71:76) cm	24(26:28:30) in
Length	40(42:46:48) cm	16(16½:18:19) in
Sleeve Seam	27(31:33:37) cm	10½(12¼:13:14½) in

Materials
5(6:7:8) 50 g/2 oz balls of *Hayfield Lugano Plain Mohair* in main colour A.
1(1:1:1) ball each in contrast colours B and C.
One pair each 4½ mm/No. 7 and 5½ mm/No. 9 knitting needles.

Tension/gauge 16 sts and 22 rows to 10 cm/4 in over st st on 5½ mm/No. 9 needles.

Abbreviations Alt-alternate; approx-approximately; beg-beginning; cm-centimetre(s); cont-continu(e)(ing); dec-decreas(e)(ing); foll-follow(s)(ing); g-gramme(s); in-inch(es); inc-increas(e)(ing); K-knit; mm-millimetre(s); No.-number; oz-ounce(s); P-purl; patt-pattern; rem-remain(s)(ing); rep-repeat(ing); st(s)-stitch(es); st st-stocking stitch/stockinette stitch; sl-slip.

BACK
** Using 4½ mm/No. 7 needles and A, cast on 50(54:58:62) sts. Cont in K2, P2 rib as foll:
1st row (right side) K2, * P2, K2, rep from * to end.
2nd row P2, * K2, P2, rep from * to end
Rep these 2 rows until work measures 6(6:7:7) cm/2½(2½:2¾:2¾) in from beg, ending with a right side row.
Next row Rib 13(15:17:19), * Inc in next st, rib 11, rep from * to last 13(15:17:19) sts, inc in next st, rib to end. 53(57:61:65) sts.
Change to 5½ mm/No. 9 needles and cont in patt as foll:
1st row (right side) Using A, K.
2nd row Using A, P.
3rd–4th rows Rep 1st–2nd rows.
5th row K2A, *1B, 3A, rep from * to last 3 sts, 1B, 2A.
6th row P2A, * K1B, P3A, rep from * to last 3 sts, K1B, P2A.
7th–10th rows Rep 1st–4th rows.
11th row * K1C, 3A, rep from * to last st, 1C.
12th row * K1C, P3A, rep from * to last st, K1C.
These 12 rows form the spot patt. Cont in patt until work measures approx 22(22:24:24) cm/8½(8½:9½:9½) in from beg, ending with a 2nd, 4th, 8th or 10th patt row. Now, beg with a K row, cont in st st.
Work 2 rows B, 4 rows C, 2 rows A.
Now cont in yoke patt. Sl all sts purl-wise with yarn on the wrong side of work.
1st row (right side) Using B, sl 1, * K3, sl 1, rep from * to end.
2nd row Using B, sl 1, P2, * sl 3, P1, rep from * to last 2 sts, sl 2.
3rd row Using C, K1, * sl 3, K1, rep from * to end.
4th row Using C, P2, * sl 1, P3, rep from * to last 3 sts, sl 1, P2.
5th row Using C, K.
6th row Using C, P.
7th row Using A, as 3rd row.
8th row Using A, as 4th row.
9th row Using A, K.
10th row Using A, P.
11th–12th rows Rep 9th–10th rows.
These 12 rows form the yoke patt. **
Cont in patt until work measures 40(42:46:48) cm/16(16½:18:19) in from beg, ending with a wrong side row.
Shape Shoulders
Next row Cast/bind off 17(18:19:20) sts, K19(21:23:25) including st used to cast/bind off, cast/bind off rem sts.

Leave these sts on a spare needle.

FRONT
Work as for Back from ** to **.
Cont in patt until work measures 14 rows less than Back to shoulder, ending with a wrong side row.
Shape Neck
Next row Patt 24(25:26:27) sts and turn leaving rem sts on a spare needle.
Complete left side of neck first.
Cast/bind off 3 sts at beg of next row, 2 sts at beg of foll alt row then dec one st at same edge on 2 foll alt rows. 17(18:19:20) sts.
Cont without shaping until work measures same as Back to shoulder.
Shape shoulder
Cast/bind off rem sts.
With right side of work facing, return to sts on spare needle. Sl centre 5(7:9:11) sts onto a stitch holder, rejoin yarn at neck edge, patt to end.
Work 1 row. Complete to match first side of neck.

SLEEVES
Using 4½ mm/No. 7 needles and A, cast on 22(22:26:26) sts. Cont in K2, P2 rib as given for back until work measures 5 cm/2 in from beg, ending with a right side row.
Next row Rib 6(5:4:3), * inc in next st, rib 4(1:2:1), rep from * to last 6(5:4:3) sts, inc in next st, rib to end. 25(29:33:37) sts.
Change to 5½ mm/No. 9 needles and cont in patt as given for Back, **at the same time**, inc one st at each end of 7th and every foll 2nd(3rd:3rd:3rd) row until there are 53(57:61:65) sts.
Cont without shaping until work measures 27(31:33:37) cm/10½(12¼:13:14½) in from beg, ending with a wrong side row.
Cast/bind off **loosely**.

TO MAKE UP
Join right shoulder seam.

COLLAR
With right side of work facing, using 4½ mm/No. 7 needles and A, K up 15 sts down left side of neck, K across 5(7:9:11) sts at centre front, K up 15 sts up right side of neck, K across 19(21:23:25) sts at back neck. 54(58:62:66) sts.
Beg with a right side row, cont in K2, P2 rib as given for Back until collar measures 18 cm/7 in from beg. Cast/bind off **loosely** in rib.
Join left shoulder seam and collar reversing seam to fold in half.
Set in sleeves, placing centre of cast/bound off edge to shoulder seam. Join side and sleeve seams.

see page 36

BOWLED OVER

Sizes

Chest	61 (66:71:76) cm	24 (26:28:30) in
Length	44 (49:52:57) cm	$17\frac{1}{2}$ ($19\frac{1}{2}$:$20\frac{1}{2}$:$22\frac{1}{2}$) in

Materials

5 (6:6:7) 50 g/2 oz balls of *Patons Diploma DK* in main colour A.
One 50 g/2 oz ball each in contrast colours B and C.
One pair each $3\frac{1}{4}$ mm/No. 4 and 4 mm/No. 6 knitting needles.

Tension/gauge 27 sts and 28 rows to 10 cm/4 in over patt on 4 mm/No. 6 needles.

> **Abbreviations** Alt-alternate; beg-beginning; cm-centimetre(s); cont-continu(e)(ing); dec-decreas(e)(ing); foll-follow(s)(ing); g-gramme(s); in-inch(es); inc-increas(e)(ing); K-knit; mm-millimetre(s); M1-make one, pick up the bar that lies between st just worked and next st and work into the back of it; No.-number; oz-ounce(s); P-purl; patt-pattern; rem- remain(s)(ing); rep-repeat(ing); st(s)-stitch(es); tog-together; TW2-twist 2, K 2nd st on left hand needle then K 1st st and slip both off needle tog; tbl-through back of loop(s).

BACK

** Using $3\frac{1}{4}$ mm/No. 4 needles and A, cast on 67 (73:77:83) sts. Cont in K1, P1 rib in stripes as foll:
1st row (right side) Using A, K1, * P1, K1, rep from * to end.
2nd row Using A, P1, * K1, P1, rep from * to end.
3rd row Using B, K.
4th row Using B, rep 2nd row.
The 3rd–4th rows form the rib. Cont in rib working 2 rows A, 2 rows C, 2 rows A, 2 rows B, 2 rows A.
Next row Using A, rep 1st row.
Next row Using A, rib 9 (12:10:13), inc in next st, * rib 1, inc in next st, rep from * to last 9 (12:10:13) sts, rib to end. 92 (98:106:112) sts.
Change to 4 mm/No. 6 needles and cont in A only. Commence patt.
1st row K.
2nd row K.
3rd row K2 (5:2:5), * P1, TW2, P1, K10 tbl, rep from * to last 6 (9:6:9) sts, P1, TW2, P1, K2 (5:2:5).
4th row P2 (5:2:5), * K1, P2, K1, P10 tbl, rep from * to last 6 (9:6:9) sts, K1, P2, K1, P2 (5:2:5).
5th–8th rows Rep 3rd–4th rows twice more.
9th row K.
10th row K.
11th row P2, K0 (3 tbl:0:3 tbl); * K7 tbl, P1, TW2, P1, K3 tbl, rep from * to last 6 (9:6:9) sts, K4 tbl (7 tbl:4 tbl:7 tbl), P2.
12th row K2, P0 (3 tbl:0:3 tbl), * P7 tbl, K1, P2, K1, P3 tbl, rep from * to last 6 (9:6:9) sts, P4 tbl (7 tbl:4 tbl:7 tbl), K2.
13th–16th rows Rep 11th–12th rows twice more.
These 16 rows form the patt. ** Cont in patt until work measures 44 (49:52:57) cm/$17\frac{1}{2}$ ($19\frac{1}{2}$:$20\frac{1}{2}$:$22\frac{1}{2}$) in from beg, ending with a wrong side row.

Shape Shoulders

Cast/bind off 28 (30:33:36) sts at beg of next 2 rows. Leave rem 36 (38:40:40) sts on a spare needle.

FRONT

Work as for Back from ** to **.
Cont in patt until work measures 27 (31:34:38) cm/ $10\frac{1}{2}$ ($12\frac{1}{4}$:$13\frac{1}{2}$:15) in from beg, ending with a wrong side row.

Shape Neck

Next row Patt 44 (47:51:54) sts, work 2 tog and turn, leaving rem sts on a spare needle.
Cont on these 45 (48:52:55) sts only for left side of neck.
Dec one st at neck edge on every foll alt row until 31 (33:35:39) sts rem, ending with a wrong side row.
Dec one st at neck edge on next and every foll 4th row

until 28 (30:33:36) sts rem.
Cont without shaping until work matches Back to shoulder, ending with a wrong side row.

Shape Shoulder

Cast off rem sts.
With right side of work facing, return to sts on spare needle. Rejoin yarn at inner edge, work 2 tog, patt to end. Complete to match first side of neck, reversing all shapings.

TO MAKE UP

Join right shoulder seam.

NECKBAND

Using $3\frac{1}{4}$ mm/No. 4 needles, A and with right side of work facing, K up 46 (48:48:50) sts down left side of neck, M1 at centre front and mark with a coloured thread, K up 46 (48:48:50) sts up right side of neck, then K2 (4:1:1), K2 tog, [K4 (2:3:3) K2 tog] 5 (7:7:7) times, K2 (4:2:2) across sts on back neck. 123 (127:129:133) sts.
1st row (wrong side) Using A, [P1, K1] to within 2 sts of marked st, P2 tog, P1, P2 tog tbl, [K1, P1] to end.
2nd row Using A, K1, [P1, K1] to within 2 sts of marked st, P2 tog, K1, P2 tog tbl, K1, [P1, K1] to end.
3rd row Using B, P to end, dec at centre as set.
4th row Using B, rep 2nd row.
Rep 3rd–4th rows, working 2 rows A, 2 rows C, 2 rows A, 2 rows B, 2 rows A.
Next row Using A, rep 1st row.
Using A, cast/bind off in rib, dec on this row as before.
Join left shoulder and neckband seam.
Mark the position of armholes 27 (31:34:38) cm/ $10\frac{1}{2}$ ($12\frac{1}{4}$:$13\frac{1}{2}$:15) in down from shoulder seams on Back and Front.

ARMBANDS

Using $3\frac{1}{4}$ mm/No. 4 needles and A, and with right side of work facing, K up 115 (119:123:127) sts evenly around armhole edge, between markers.
1st row (wrong side) Using A, P1, * K1, P1, rep from * to end.
2nd row Using A, K1, * P1, K1, rep from * to end.
3rd row Using B, P.
4th row Using B, rep 2nd row.
Rep 3rd–4th rows, working 2 rows A, 2 rows C, 2 rows A, 2 rows B, 2 rows A.
Next row Using A, rep 1st row.
Using A, cast/bind off in rib.
Join side seams, overlap front armband over back diagonally and catch down row ends neatly.

see page 37

DEMURE AND DOTTY

Sizes
Chest	61(66:71:77) cm	24(26:28:30) in
Length	40(44:47:51) cm	16(17½:18½:20) in
Sleeve Seam	27(31:35:39) cm	10½(12¼:13¾:15½) in

Materials
3(3:4:4) 50 g/2 oz balls of *Sunbeam St Ives* 4 ply in main colour A.
1(1:1:1) ball each in contrast colours B and C.
One pair each 2¾ mm/No. 2 and 3¼ mm/No. 4 knitting needles.
Crochet hook.
2 buttons.

Tension/gauge 29 sts and 36 rows to 10 cm/4 in over patt on 3¼ mm/No. 4 needles.

Abbreviations Approx-approximately; alt-alternate; beg-beginning; cont-continu(e)(ing); cm-centimetre(s); dec-decreas(e)(ing); foll-follow(s)(ing); g-gramme(s); in-inch(es); inc-increas(e)(ing); K-knit; mm-millimetre(s); No.-number; oz-ounce(s); P-purl; patt-pattern; rem-remain(s)(ing); rep-repeat(ing); st(s)-stitch(es); sl-slip.

BACK
** Using 2¾ mm/No. 2 needles and A, cast on 76(84:90:98) sts. Cont in K1, P1 rib until work measures 5(5:6:6) cm/2(2:2½:2½) in from beg, ending with a right side row.
Next row Rib 2(6:9:4), * inc in next st, rib 3(3:3:4), rep from * to last 2(6:9:4) sts, inc in next st, rib to end. 95(103:109:117) sts.
Change to 3¼ mm/No. 4 needles and cont in patt as foll:
1st row (right side) K.
2nd row P.
3rd row K2(0:0:1)A, * 3A, 1B, 2A, rep from * to last 3(1:1:2) sts, 3(1:1:2) A.
4th row P3(1:1:2) A, * P2A, K1B, P3A, rep from * to last 2(0:0:1) sts, P2(0:0:1) A.
5th row K.
6th row P.
7th row K2(0:0:1) A, * 1C, 5A, rep from * to last 3(1:1:2) sts, 1C, 2(0:0:1)A.
8th row P2(0:0:1) A, K1C, * P5A, K1C, rep from * to last 2(0:0:1) sts, P2(0:0:1) A.
These 8 rows form the patt. Cont in patt until work measures approx 27(30:32:34) cm/10½(12:12½:13½) in from beg, ending with a 2nd(2nd:6th:4th) patt row.
Shape Armholes
Keeping patt correct, cast/bind off 2 sts at beg of next 2 rows. Dec one st at each end of next and every foll alt row until 67(71:77:83) sts rem. **
Cont without shaping until work measures 40(44:47:51) cm/16(17½:18½:20) in from beg, ending with a wrong side row.
Shape Shoulders
Cast/bind off 10(10:11:12) sts at beg of next 2 rows, then 9(9:10:12) sts at beg of foll 2 rows. Leave rem 29(33:35:35) sts on a spare needle.

FRONT
Work as given for Back from ** to **.
Cont without shaping until work measures 35(39:42:46) cm/13¾(15½:16½:18) in from beg, ending with a wrong side row.
Shape Neck
Next row Patt 28(29:32:34) sts and turn, leaving rem sts on a spare needle.
Complete left side of neck first.
Dec one st at neck edge on every row until 19(19:21:24) sts rem.
Cont without shaping until work measures same as Back to shoulder, ending at armhole edge.
Shape Shoulder
Cast/bind off 10(10:11:12) sts at beg of next row. Work 1 row. Cast/bind off rem 9(9:10:12) sts.

With right side of work facing, return to sts on spare needle. Sl centre 11(13:13:15) sts onto a stitch holder, rejoin yarn at neck edge, patt to end.
Complete to match left side of neck.

SLEEVES
Using 2¾ mm/No. 2 needles and A, cast on 44(46:48:50) sts. Cont in K1, P1 rib until work measures 4(4:5:5) cm/1½(1½:2:2) in from beg, ending with a right side row.
Next row Rib 2(5:4:7), * inc in next st, rib 1, rep from * to last 2(5:4:7) sts, inc in next st, rib to end. 65(65:69:69) sts.
Change to 3¼ mm/No. 4 needles. Cont in patt as given for 1st(1st:4th:4th) size of Back, **at the same time**, inc one st at each end of 5th and every foll 8th row until there are 71(73:79:85) sts.
Cont without shaping until work measures 27(31:35:39) cm/10½(12¼:13¾:15½) in from beg, ending with a wrong side row.
Shape Top/Cap
Cast/bind off 2 sts at beg of next 2 rows. Dec one st at each end of next and every foll alt row until 35(35:33:41) sts rem, then at each end of every row until 21(21:23:23) sts rem. Cast/bind off.

TO MAKE UP
Join right shoulder seam.

COLLAR
With right side of work facing, using 2¾ mm/No. 2 needles and A, K up 26(27:28:29) sts down left side of neck, K across 11(13:13:15) at centre front inc 2 sts evenly, K up 26(27:28:29) sts up right side of neck, K across 29(33:35:35) sts at back neck, inc 6 sts evenly. 100(108:112:116) sts.
Cont in K1, P1 rib until collar measures 3 cm/1¼ in from beg, ending with a wrong side row.
Divide Front Collar
Next row Rib 33(35:36:38) sts, turn and leave rem sts on a spare needle.
Complete this side of collar first.
Rib 10 rows.
Dec one st at front edge on next and foll 2 alt rows, then dec one st at same edge on foll 4 rows. Cast/bind off in rib.
With right side of work facing, return to sts on spare needle. Rejoin yarn to rem 67(73:76:78) sts, inc in first st, rib to end.
Complete to match first side of collar.
Join left shoulder and collar seam.
Join side and sleeve seams. Set in sleeves gathering fullness at shoulder.

CONTRAST COLLAR
Using 2¾ mm/No. 2 needles and C, cast on 112(120:124:128) sts. Cont in K1, P1 rib until collar measures 2 cm/¾ in from beg.
Divide Collar
Next row Rib 56(60:62:64) sts and turn, leaving rem sts on a spare needle.
Complete this side of collar first.
Rib 13 rows.
Dec one st at front edge on next and 3 foll alt rows, then dec one st at same edge on 5 foll rows. Cast/bind off in rib.
Return to sts on spare needle. Rejoin yarn at inner edge, inc in first st, rib to end. 57(61:63:64) sts.
Complete to match first side of collar.
Using crochet hook work 1 row of double crochet/single crochet around outer edges of collar. Work 2 button loops on one back edge. Sew on buttons to correspond.

see page 38

PUNCHY PRIMARIES

Sizes

Chest	61(66:71:76) cm	24(26:28:30) in
Length	41(43:45:47) cm	16¼(17:17¾:18½) in
Sleeve Seam	30(32:34:36) cm	12(12½:13½:14¼) in

Materials

6(7:8:8) 50 g/2 oz balls of *Scheepjeswol Superwash Zermatt* in main colour A.
One 50 g/2 oz ball in each of 3 contrast colours B, C and D.
One pair each 3¼ mm/No. 4 and 4 mm/No. 6 knitting needles.
3 buttons.

Tension/gauge 22 sts and 28 rows to 10 cm/4 in over st st on 4 mm/No. 6 needles.

Abbreviations Alt-alternate; beg-beginning; cm-centimetre(s); cont-continu(e)(ing); dec-decreas(e)(ing); foll-follow(s)(ing); g-gramme(s); in-inch(es); inc-increas(e)(ing); K-knit; mm-millimetre(s); No.-number; oz-ounce(s); P-purl; rem-remain(s)(ing); rep-repeat(ing); st(s)-stitch(es); st st-stocking stitch/stockinette stitch.

BACK

** Using 3¼ mm/No. 4 needles and B, cast on 70(76:82:88) sts.
Cont in K1, P1 rib until work measures 5 cm/2 in from beg.
Next row Rib 10(9:9:12), [inc in next st, rib 6(7:8:8)] 7 times, inc in next st, rib to end. 78(84:90:96) sts.
Change to 4 mm/No. 6 needles and A. Beg with a K row cont in st st until work measures 25(26:27:28) cm/10(10¼:10½:11) in from beg, ending with a P row.

Shape Armholes
Cast off 3(4:5:6) sts at beg of next 2 rows. 72(76:80:84) sts. **
Cont in st st until work measures 41(43:45:47) cm/16¼(17:17¾:18½) in from beg, ending with a P row.

Shape Shoulders
Cast/bind off 7(8:9:9) sts at beg of next 2 rows, 8(8:8:9) sts at beg of foll 2 rows and 8 sts at beg of next 2 rows.
Leave rem 26(28:30:32) sts on a spare needle.

FRONT

Work as for Back from ** to **.
Cont in st st until work measures 27(29:30:32) cm/10½(11½:12:12¾) in from beg, ending with a P row.

Divide for Neck
Next row K33(35:37:39) sts and turn, leaving rem sts on a spare needle.
Cont on these sts for left side of neck until work measures 19(19:21:21) rows less than Back to shoulder, ending with a K row.

Shape Neck
Cast off 2(2:3:3) sts at beg of next row, then dec one st at neck edge on next and every foll alt row until 23(24:25:26) sts rem.
Cont without shaping. Work 3(1:3:1) rows, ending with a P row.

Shape Shoulder
Cast/bind off 7(8:9:9) sts at beg of next row and 8(8:8:9) sts at beg of foll alt row. Work 1 row. Cast/bind off rem 8 sts.
With right side of work facing, return to sts on spare needle. Rejoin yarn at neck edge, cast/bind off 6 sts, K to end.
Complete to match first side of neck, reversing all shapings.

SLEEVES

Using 3¼ mm/No. 4 needles and C, cast on 38(42:44:48) sts.
Cont in K1, P1 rib until work measures 5 cm/2 in from beg.
Next row Rib 8(8:6:8), [inc in next st, rib 6(7:5:5)] 3(3:5:5) times, inc in next st, rib to end. 42(46:50:54) sts.

Change to 4 mm/No. 6 needles and A. Beg with a K row cont in st st inc one st at each end of next and every foll 4th(5th:5th:5th) row until there are 70(74:80:84) sts.
Cont without shaping until work measures 30(32:34:36) cm/12(12½:13½:14¼) in from beg.
Mark each end of last row with a coloured thread.
Work a further 4(6:7:8) rows.
Cast/bind off **loosely**.

BUTTONBAND

Using 3¼ mm/No. 4 needles and B, and with right side of work facing, K up 21 sts down left neck opening edge.
Cont in K1, P1 rib as foll:
1st row (wrong side) P1, * K1, P1, rep from * to end.
2nd row K1, * P1, K1, rep from * to end.
Rep the last 2 rows twice more, then the 1st row again.
Cast/bind off in rib.

BUTTONHOLE BAND

Using 3¼ mm/No. 4 needles and C, and with right side of work facing, K up 21 sts up right neck opening edge.
Work 3 rows K1, P1 rib as for buttonband.
Next row Rib 3 [cast/bind off 2 sts, rib the next 3 sts] twice, cast/bind off 2 sts, rib to end.
Next row Rib to end, casting on 2 sts over those cast/bound off in previous row.
Work 2 more rows rib. Cast/bind off in rib.

TO MAKE UP

Join shoulder seams.

COLLAR

Using 3¼ mm/No. 4 needles and D, and with right side of work facing, K up 24(24:27:27) sts across buttonhole band, up right front neck, K26(28:30:32) sts from back neck, K up 24(24:27:27) down left front neck across buttonband. 74(76:84:86) sts.
Cont in K1, P1 rib until collar measures 2 cm/¾ in from beg.
Next row Rib 10, [inc in next st] 54(56:64:66) times, rib to end. 128(132:148:152) sts.
Cont in rib until collar measures 8(8:9:9) cm/3¼(3¼:3½:3½) in from beg.
Cast/bind off in rib **loosely**.
Set in sleeves, matching coloured threads to side seams, joining final rows of sleeve to sts cast/bound off at underarm. Join side and sleeve seams. Sew short ends of bands to centre front. Sew on buttons.

see page 40

DIAMOND DANDY

Sizes

Chest	61(66:71:76) cm	24(26:28:30) in
Length	41(41:43:43) cm	16¼(16¼:17:17) in
Sleeve Seam	30(34:38:42) cm	12(13½:15:16½) in

Materials

4(4:5:5) 50 g/2 oz balls of *Hayfield Grampian DK* in main colour (A).
1(1:1:1) ball each in contrast colours B, C and D.
One pair each 3¼ mm/No. 4 and 4 mm/No. 6 knitting needles.
3 buttons.

Tension/gauge 22 sts and 26 rows to 10 cm/4 in over st st on 4 mm/No. 6 needles.

Abbreviations Beg-beginning; cm-centimetre(s); cont-continu(e)(ing); dec-decreas(e)(ing); foll-follow(s)(ing); g-gramme(s); in-inch(es); inc-increas(e)(ing); K-knit; mm-millimetre(s); No.-number; oz-ounce(s); P-purl; rem-remain(s)(ing); rep-repeat(ing); st(s)-stitch(es); st st-stocking stitch/stockinette stitch; sl-slip.

BACK

** Using 3¼ mm/No. 4 needles and A, cast on 66(72:78:84) sts. Cont in K1, P1 rib until work measures 6 cm/2½ in from beg, ending with a right side row.
Next row Rib 3(6:3:6), *inc in next st, rib 4(4:5:5), rep from * to last 3(6:3:6) sts, inc in next st, rib to end. 79(85:91:97) sts.
Change to 4 mm/No. 6 needles. Beg with a K row cont in st st working from chart 1. Read K rows from right to left and P rows from left to right. Work 5 rows, ending with a K row.
Cont in A only and st st until work measures 19(19:20:20) cm/7½(7½:8:8) in from beg, ending with a P row.
Now commence working from chart 2 as foll:
Next row K5(8:11:14) A, work 1st row of chart, K5(8:11:14) A.
Next row P5(8:11:14) A, work 2nd row of chart, P5(8:11:14) A. **
Keeping chart correct, cont as set until work measures 41(41:43:43) cm/16¼(16¼:17:17) in from beg, ending with a P row.

Shape Shoulders

Cast/bind off 13(14:15:16) sts at beg of next 4 rows.
Leave rem 27(29:31:33) sts on a spare needle.

FRONT

Work as given for Back from ** to **.
Keeping chart correct, cont as set until work measures 10(10:14:14) rows less than Back to shoulder shaping, ending with a P row.

Shape Neck

Next row Work 34(36:38:40) sts and turn, leaving rem sts on a spare needle.
Complete left side of neck first.
Dec one st at neck edge on every row until 26(28:30:32) sts rem.
Cont without shaping, work 1(1:5:5) rows.

Shape Shoulder

Cast/bind off 13(14:15:16) sts at beg of next row.
Work 1 row. Cast/bind off the rem 13(14:15:16) sts.
With right side of work facing, return to sts on spare needle. Sl centre 11(13:15:17) sts onto a stitch holder, rejoin yarn at neck edge, work to end.
Complete to match left side of neck.

SLEEVES

Using 3¼ mm/No. 4 needles and A, cast on 37(39:41:43) sts.
1st row (right side) K1, * P1, K1, rep from * to end.
2nd row P1, * K1, P1, rep from * to end.
Rep these 2 rows until work measures 5 cm/2 in from beg, ending with a right side row.
Next row Rib 3(4:3:4), * inc in next st, rib 5(5:6:6), rep from * to last 4(5:3:4) sts, inc in next st, rib to end. 43(45:47:49) sts.
Change to 4 mm/No. 6 needles. Beg with a K row cont in st st working from chart 1. Work 5 rows.
Cont in A only and st st, inc one st at each end of next and every foll 6th(6th:6th:7th) row until there are 63(67:71:75) sts.
Cont without shaping until work measures 30(34:38:42) cm/12(13½:15:16½) in from beg, ending with a P row.
Cast/bind off **loosely**.

TO MAKE UP

Join right shoulder seam.

NECKBAND

Using 3¼ mm/No. 4 needles and A, and with right side of work facing, K up 17(17:18:18) sts down left side of neck, K across 11(13:15:17) sts at centre front, K up 17(17:18:18) sts up right side of neck then K across 27(29:31:33) sts at back neck. 72(76:82:86) sts.
Cont in K1, P1 rib until neckband measures 5 cm/2 in from beg, ending with a wrong side row.
Cast/bind off **loosely** in rib.
Fold neckband in half onto wrong side and catch down.

BUTTONHOLE BAND

With right side of work facing, using 3¼ mm/No. 4 needles and A, K up 31(32:33:34) sts from left front shoulder edge and neckband.
Next row K1(0:1:0), * P1, K1, rep from * to end.
Next row Rib 9(10:9:10), * cast/bind off 3 sts, rib 5(5:6:6) including st used to cast/bind off, rep from * ending last rep rib 3.
Next row Rib to end, casting on 3 sts over those cast/bound off in previous row.
Rib 3 rows. Cast/bind off **loosely** in rib.

BUTTONBAND

With right side of work facing, using 3¼ mm/No. 4 needles and A, K up 31(32:33:34) sts from left back shoulder edge and neckband.
Work 3 rows K1, P1 rib as given for buttonhole band.
Cast/bind off **loosely** in rib.
Press work. Using chart, Swiss darn diamonds in D.
Catch together left shoulder seam at armhole edge, lapping buttonhole band over buttonband. Set in sleeves, matching centre of cast/bound off edge to shoulder seam. Join side and sleeve seams.
Sew on buttons.

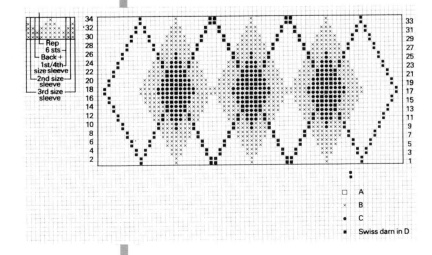

□	A
✗	B
•	C
■	Swiss darn in D

see page 41

FISHERMAN'S RIB

Sizes

Chest	61(66:71:76) cm	24(26:28:30) in
Length	42(46:49:53) cm	16½(18:19¼:21) in
Sleeve Seam	27(31:35:43) cm	10½(12¼:13¾:17) in

Materials

6(6:7:7) 50 g/2 oz balls of *Phildar Detente* in main colour A.
Two 50 g/2 oz balls in contrast colour B.
One pair each 3 mm/No. 3 and 3¾ mm/No. 5 knitting needles.

Tension/gauge 20 sts and 42 rows to 10 cm/4 in over patt using 3¾ mm/No. 5 needles.

Abbreviations Beg-beginning; cm-centimetre(s); cont-continu(e)(ing); dec-decreas(e)(ing); foll-follow(s)(ing); g-gramme(s); in-inch(es); inc-increas(e)(ing); K-knit; K1B-knit next st in the row below; mm-millimetre(s); No.-number; oz-ounce; P-purl; patt-pattern; rem-remain(s)(ing); rep-repeat (ing); st(s)-stitch(es); st st-stocking stitch/stockinette stitch; sl-slip.

BACK
** Using 3 mm/No. 3 needles and A, cast on 77(83:87:93) sts. Cont in K1, P1 rib as foll:
1st row (right side) P1, * K1, P1, rep from * to end.
2nd row K1, * P1, K1, rep from * to end.
Rep the last 2 rows until work measures 7(7:8:8) cm/2¾(2¾:3:3) in from beg, ending with a wrong side row. Change to 3¾ mm/No. 5 needles and cont in patt.
1st row (right side) K.
2nd row K1, * P1, K1B, rep from * to last 2 sts, P1, K1.
These 2 rows form the patt. Cont in patt until work measures 28(31:33:36) cm/11(12¼:13:14¼) in from beg, ending with a wrong side row. **
Change to B.
Cont in patt as set until work measures 42(46:49:53) cm/16½(18:19¼:21) in from beg, ending with a wrong side row.
Shape Shoulders
Cast/bind off 13(14:14:15) sts at beg of next 4 rows.
Leave the rem 25(27:31:33) sts on a spare needle.

FRONT
Work as for Back from ** to **.
Change to B.
Cont in patt as set until work measures 38(41:44:48) cm/

15(16¼:17¼:19) in from beg, ending with a wrong side row.
Shape Neck
Next row Patt 34(36:36:38) sts and turn, leaving rem sts on a spare needle.
Cont on these sts only for left side of neck.
Dec one st at neck edge on every row until 26(28:28:30) sts rem.
Cont without shaping until work matches Back to shoulder, ending at armhole edge.
Shape Shoulder
Cast/bind off 13(14:14:15) sts at beg of next row.
Work 1 row. Cast/bind off rem 13(14:14:15) sts.
With right side of work facing, return to sts on spare needle. Sl centre 9(11:15:17) sts onto a holder, rejoin yarn at inner edge, patt to end. Complete as for first side of neck.

SLEEVES
Using 3 mm/No. 3 needles and A, cast on 37(39:41:43) sts. Cont in K1, P1 rib as for Back until work measures 4(4:5:5) cm/1½(1½:2:2) in from beg, ending with a wrong side row.
Change to 3¾ mm/No. 5 needles and cont in patt as for Back, inc one st at each end of 3rd and every foll 7th (7th:7th:8th) row until there are 61(67:71:73) sts.
Cont without shaping until work measures 27 (31:35:43) cm/10½(12¼:13¾:17) in from beg, ending with a wrong side row.
Cast/bind off **loosely**.

TO MAKE UP
Join right shoulder seam.

NECKBAND
Using 3 mm/No. 3 needles and B, and with right side of work facing, K up 19(20:20:21) sts down left side of neck, K across 9(11:15:17) sts from front inc 2 sts evenly, K up 19(20:20:21) sts up right side of neck, K across 25(27:31:33) sts from back neck inc 6 sts evenly, 80(86:94:100) sts. Cont in K1, P1 rib until neckband measures 5(5:7:7) cm/2(2:2¾:2¾) in from beg. Cast/bind off **loosely** in rib.
Join left shoulder and neckband. Fold neckband in half onto wrong side and catch down. Set in sleeves, placing centre of cast/bound off edge to shoulder seams. Join side and sleeve seams.

see page 42

DEERSTALKER

Sizes

Chest	61(66:71:76) cm	24(26:28:30) in
Length	35(39:41:43) cm	13¾(15½:16:17) in
Sleeve Seam	32(37:42:47) cm	12½(14½:16½:18½) in

Materials

4(4:4:5) 50 g/2 oz balls of *Wendy Shetland DK* in main colour A.
1(2:2:2) balls in contrast colour B.
1(1:1:1) ball each in contrast colours C and D.
One pair each 3¼ mm/No. 4 and 4 mm/No. 6 knitting needles.

Tension/gauge 24 sts and 29 rows to 10 cm/4 in over patt on 4 mm/No. 6 needles.

Abbreviations Alt-alternate; beg-beginning; cm-centimetre(s); cont-continu(e)(ing); foll-follow(s)(ing); inc-increas(e)(ing); K-knit; mm-millimetre(s); No.-number; oz-ounce; P-purl; rem-remain(s)(ing); rep-repeat(ing); st(s)-stitch(es); st st-stocking stitch/stockinette stitch; sl-slip.

BACK
** Using 3¼ mm/No. 4 needles and B, cast on 68(74:80:86) sts. Cont in K1, P1 rib until work measures 5 cm/2 in from beg.
Next row Rib 10(7:10:7), [inc in next st, rib 3(4:4:5)] 12 times, inc in next st, rib to end. 81(87:93:99) sts.
Change to 4 mm/No. 6 needles and C.
K 2 rows.
Change to A and beg with a K row cont in st st working from chart, beg at 11th(1st:1st:1st) row. Read K rows from right to left and P rows from left to right. Strand yarn not in use *loosely* across back of work and twist yarns when changing colour to avoid a hole. **
Cont until 86(96:102:108) rows have been worked from chart, ending with a P row.
Shape Shoulders
Cast/bind off 9(10:11:11) sts at beg of next 2 rows, 9(10:10:11) sts at beg of foll 2 rows and 9(10:10:10) sts at beg of next 2 rows. Leave rem 27(27:31:35) sts on a spare needle.

FRONT
Work as for Back from ** to **.
Cont until 76(86:92:98) rows have been worked from

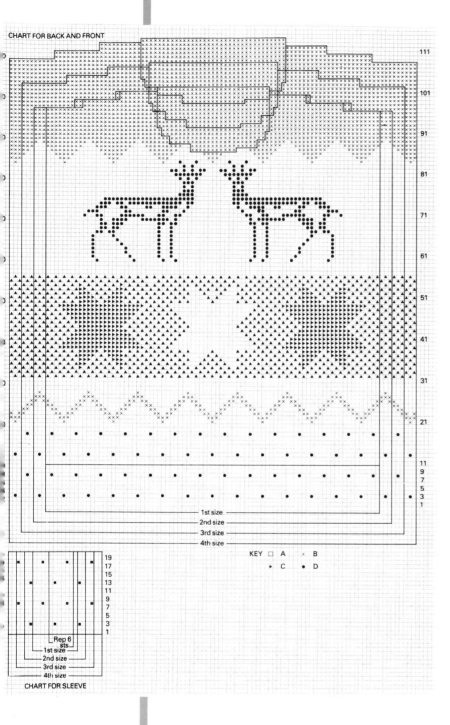

CHART FOR BACK AND FRONT

KEY □ A × B ► C • D

CHART FOR SLEEVE

chart, ending with a P row.

Shape Neck

Next row Work 35(38:40:42) sts and turn, leaving rem sts on a spare needle.

Complete left side of neck first.

Cast/bind off 5(5:5:6) sts at beg of next row and 2(2:3:3) sts at beg of 2 foll alt rows. 18(19:21:22:) sts.

Cont without shaping until work matches Back to shoulder, ending at armhole edge.

Shape Shoulder

Cast/bind off 9(10:11:11) sts at beg of next row and 9(10:10:11) sts at beg of foll alt row. Work 1 row.

Cast/bind off rem 9(10:10:10) sts.

With right side of work facing, return to sts on spare needle. Sl centre 11(11:13:15) sts onto a stitch holder, rejoin yarn at neck edge and work to end.

Work 1 row.

Complete as for first side of neck.

SLEEVES

Using 3¼ mm/No. 4 needles and B, cast on 41(43:45:47) sts. Cont in K1, P1 rib as foll:

1st row (right side) K1, * P1, K1, rep from * to end.

2nd row P1, * K1, P1, rep from * to end.

Rep these 2 rows for 5 cm/2 in, ending with a right side row.

Next row Rib 8(7:4:7), * inc in next st, rib 4(3:3:2), rep from * to last 8(8:5:7) sts, inc in next st, rib to end. 47(51:55:59) sts.

Change to 4 mm needles and C.

K 2 rows.

Change to A and beg with a K row cont in st st working from chart. **At the same time**, inc one st at each end of 5th and every foll 6th row until there are 57(61:65:69) sts, then at each end of every foll 6th row until there are 69(73:77:81) sts.

Cont without shaping until work measures 31(36:41:46) cm/12¼(14¼:16¼:18) in from beg, ending with a P row.

Change to C, K 2 rows.

Change to A, K 1 row. Cast/bind off **loosely**.

TO MAKE UP

Join right shoulder seam.

NECKBAND

Using 3¼ mm/No. 4 needles and B, and with right side of work facing, K up 24 sts down left side of neck, K across 11(11:13:15) sts at centre front, K up 24 sts up right side of neck and K across 27(27:31:35) sts on back neck. 86(86:92:98) sts.

Cont in K1, P1 rib until neckband measures 2·5 cm/1 in from beg.

Cast off in rib.

Join left shoulder and neckband. Set in sleeves, placing centre of cast/bound off edge to shoulder seam. Join side and sleeve seams.

see page 43

ALL WEATHER WOOLLY

Sizes

Chest	61 (66:71:76) cm	24 (26:28:30) in
Length	47 (51:55:58) cm	18½ (20:21½:23) in
Sleeve Seam	27 (31:34:38) cm	10¾ (12¼:13¾:15) in

Materials

9(10:11:12) 50 g/2 oz balls of *Emu Superwash DK*.

One pair each 3¼ mm/No. 4 and 4 mm/No. 6 knitting needles.

3¼ mm/No. 4 and 3¾ mm/No. 5 circular knitting needles.

Cable needle.

Tension/gauge 24 sts and 32 rows to 10 cm/4 in over rev st st on 4 mm/No. 6 needles.

Abbreviations Alt-alternate; beg-beginning; cm-centimetre(s); cont-continu(e)(ing); Cr2R-cross 2 right, K2 tog but do not sl sts off needle, K the 1st st again, then sl sts off needle tog; Cr2L- cross 2 left, K tbl 2nd st on left hand needle, K2 tog tbl 1st and 2nd sts and sl off needle tog; C6F-cable 6 front, sl next 3 sts onto cable needle and hold at front of work, K3 then K3 from cable needle; dec-decreas(e)(ing); foll-follow(s)(ing); g-gramme(s); in-inch(es); inc-increas(e)(ing); K-knit; mm-millimetre(s); MB-make bobble, [K1, yfwd/yo, K1, yfwd/yo, K1] all into next st, turn K5, turn P5, turn K1, sl 1, K2 tog, psso, K1, turn P3 tog; No.-number; oz-ounce(s); P-purl; patt-pattern; psso-pass slipped st over; rem-remain(s)(ing); rep-repeat(ing); rev st st-reverse stocking/stockinette st; sl-slip; st(s)-stitch(es); tog-together; yfwd/yo-yarn forward.

CABLE PANEL—worked over 17 sts
1st row (wrong side) K2, P13, K2.
2nd row P2, K2, Cr2L, K2, Cr2R, K5, P2.
3rd and foll alt rows As 1st.
4th row P2, K3, Cr2L, Cr2R, K6, P2.
6th row P2, K4, Cr2L, K4, MB, K2, P2.
8th row P2, K5, Cr2L, K2, Cr2R, K2, P2.
10th row P2, K6, Cr2L, Cr2R, K3, P2.
12th row P2, K2, MB, K4, Cr2R, K4, P2.
These 12 rows form the cable panel.

BACK
** Using 3¼ mm/No. 4 needles, cast on 78(84:90:96) sts.
Cont in K1, P1 rib until work measures 5 cm/2 in from
beg, ending with a wrong side row.
Next row Rib 3(6:9:12), * work twice into next st, rib 2,
rep from * to last 3(6:9:12) sts, work twice into next st, rib
to end. 103(109:115:121) sts.
Change to 4 mm/No. 6 needles and commence patt.
1st row (wrong side) K14(17:20:23), P6, [work 1st row
of cable panel, P6] 3 times, K14(17:20:23).
2nd row P14(17:20:23), C6F, [work 2nd row of cable
panel, C6F] 3 times, P14(17:20:23).
3rd row K14(17:20:23), P6, [work 3rd row of cable
panel, P6] 3 times, K14(17:20:23).
4th row P14(17:20:23), K6, [work 4th row of cable
panel, K6] 3 times, P14(17:20:23).
These 4 rows establish the patt for the edge sts. **
Keeping edge sts and cable panel correct, cont until work
measures 47(51:55:58) cm/18½(20:21½:23) in from beg,
ending with a wrong side row.
Shape Shoulders
Next row Cast/bind off 34(36:38:40) sts, patt
35(37:39:41) and sl onto a spare needle, cast/bind off
rem sts.

FRONT
Work as for Back from ** to **.
Keeping edge sts and cable panel correct, cont until
work measures 39(43:47:50) cm/15¼(17:18½:19¾) in
from beg, ending with a wrong side row.
Shape Neck
Next row Patt 45(47:49:51) sts and turn leaving rem sts
on a spare needle.
Cont on these sts only for left side of neck.
Dec one st at neck edge on every row until 34(36:38:40)
sts rem.
Cont without shaping until work matches Back to
shoulder, ending at armhole edge.
Shape Shoulder

Cast/bind off rem sts.
With right side of work facing, return to sts on spare
needle. Sl centre 13(15:17:19) sts onto a holder, rejoin
yarn to neck edge and patt to end. Complete to match first
side of neck.

SLEEVES
Using 3¼ mm/No. 4 needles, cast on 40(42:44:48) sts.
Cont in K1, P1 rib until work measures 5(5:6:6) cm/
2(2:2½:2½) in from beg, ending with a wrong side row.
Next row [Work twice into next st] 6(8:8:6) times, * rib
1, work twice into next st, rep from * to last 8(8:10:8)
sts, rib 1, [work twice into next st] 7(7:9:7) times.
66(70:74:78) sts.
Change to 4 mm/No. 6 needles and commence patt.
1st row (wrong side) K7(9:11:13), [P6, work 1st row of
cable panel] twice, K7(9:11:13).
2nd row P7(9:11:13), [C6F, work 2nd row of cable
panel] twice, C6F, P7(9:11:13).
These 2 rows establish the patt. Keeping edge sts as for
Back and cable panel correct, cont in patt inc one st at
each end of 5th and every foll 8th row until there are
72(78:82:88) sts, then at each end of every foll 6th row
until there are 76(86:94:104) sts and every foll 4th row
until there are 92(98:104:110) sts.
Cont without shaping, work 4 rows.
Cast/bind off.

TO MAKE UP
Join shoulder seams.

COLLAR
Using 3¼ mm/No. 4 circular needle, with right side of
work facing, beg at centre of front neck sts on holder, K
across 7(8:9:10) sts, inc 2 sts evenly, K up 24(26:26:28)
sts up right side of neck, K across 35(37:39:41) sts on
back neck, inc 9 sts evenly, K up 24(26:26:28) sts down
left side of neck, then K across rem 6(7:8:9) sts on holder,
inc 3 sts evenly. 110(118:122:130) sts.
Work in rounds of K1, P1 rib. Work 7 rounds.
Change to 3¾ mm/No. 5 circular needle. Cont to work in
rows of K1, P1 rib as foll:
1st row Work twice in 1st st, rib to last st, K1.
2nd row K1, rib to last st, K1.
Rep the last row 13 times more. Cast off in rib **loosely**.
Mark position of armholes 15(17:18:19) cm/
6(6¾:7¼:7½) in down from shoulder seams. Set in sleeves
between markers, gathering or pleating at shoulder to fit.
Join side and sleeve seams.

see page 44

LACY BOAT NECK

Sizes

Chest	61–66(71–76) cm	24–26(28–30) in
Length	40(44) cm	15¾(17½) in
Sleeve Seam	33(37) cm	13(14½) in

Materials
8(10) 50 g/2 oz balls of *Phildar Detente Cotton*.
One pair each 3 mm/No. 3 and 3¾ mm/No. 5 knitting
needles.

Tension/gauge 24 sts and 32 rows to 10 cm/4 in over
patt on 3¾ mm/No. 5 needles.

Abbreviations Beg-beginning; cm-centimetre(s);
cont-continu(e)(ing); foll-follow(s)(ing); g-
gramme(s); in-inch(es); inc-increase(e)(ing); K-knit;
mm-millimetre(s); No.-number; oz-ounce(s); P-purl;
patt-pattern; psso-pass slipped stitch over; rem-re-
main(s)(ing); rep-repeat(ing); st(s)-stitch(es); sl-
slip; tog-together; yfwd/yo-yarn forward.

BACK
Using 3 mm/No. 3 needles, cast on 75(87) sts. Cont in
K1, P1 rib as foll:
1st row (right side) P1, * K1, P1, rep from * to end.

2nd row K1, * P1, K1, rep from * to end.
Rep the last 2 rows until work measures 5 cm/2 in from
beg, ending with a 1st row.
Next row Rib 5(7), * inc in next st, rib 6(7), rep from * to
end. 85(97) sts.
Change to 3¾ mm/No. 5 needles and commence patt.
1st row (right side) K1, * yfwd/yo, K2, P7, K2, yfwd/yo,
K1, rep from * to end.
2nd row P4, * K2, sl 1, K2 tog, psso, K2, P7, rep from *
ending last rep P4.
3rd row K2, * yfwd/yo, K2, P5, K2, yfwd/yo, K3, rep
from * ending last rep K2.
4th row P5, * K1, sl 1, K2 tog, psso, K1, P9, rep from *
ending last rep P5.
5th row K3, * yfwd/yo, K2, P3, K2, yfwd/yo, K5, rep
from * ending last rep K3.
6th row P6, * sl 1, K2 tog, psso, P11, rep from * ending
last rep P6.
7th row P4, * K2, yfwd/yo, K1, yfwd/yo, K2, P7, rep
from * ending last rep P4.
8th row K2 tog, * K2, P7, K2, sl 1, K2 tog, psso, rep from
* to last 13 sts, K2, P7, K2, K2 tog.
9th row P3, * K2, yfwd/yo, K3, yfwd/yo, K2, P5, rep
from * ending last rep P3.
10th row K2 tog, * K1, P9, K1, sl 1, K2 tog, psso, rep

from * to last 13 sts, K1, P9, K1, K2 tog.
11th row P2, * K2, yfwd/yo, K5, yfwd/yo, K2, P3, rep from * ending last rep P2.
12th row: K2 tog, * P11, sl 1, K2 tog, psso, rep from * to last 13 sts, P11, K2 tog.
These 12 rows form the patt. Rep these 12 rows 7(8) times more.
Change to 3 mm/No. 3 needles. Cont in K1, P1 rib as before for a further 5 cm/2 in.
Cast/bind off **loosely** in rib.

FRONT
Work as for Back.

SLEEVES
Using 3 mm/No. 3 needles, cast on 41(45) sts. Cont in

K1, P1 rib as for Back until work measures 5 cm/2 in from beg, ending with a 1st row.
Next row Rib 6(8), * inc in next st, rib 3(8), rep from * to last 7(10) sts, inc in next st, rib to end. 49 sts.
Change to 3¾ mm/No. 5 needles and commence patt as for Back. Inc and work into patt, one st at each end of 3rd and every foll 5th row until there are 83(89) sts. Cont without shaping. Work 7(4) rows, so ending with a 6th patt row.
Cast/bind off **loosely**.

TO MAKE UP
Join shoulder seams for 10(12) cm/4(4¾) in, leaving rem for neck opening. Set in sleeves, placing centre of cast/bound off edge to shoulder seams. Join side and sleeve seams.

---

see page 45

SOLO SWEATER

Sizes
Chest	61(68:71:78) cm	24(27:28:31) in
Length	47(51:55:59) cm	18½(20:21¾:23¼) in
Sleeve Seam	30(32:34:36) cm	12(12½:13½:14¼) in

Materials
8(9:9:10) 50 g/2 oz balls of *Sunbeam Pure New Wool DK*.
One pair each 3¼ mm/No. 4 and 4 mm/No. 6 knitting needles.
3¼ mm/No. 4 circular knitting needle.

Tension/gauge
24 sts and 38 rows to 10 cm/4 in over patt on 4 mm/No. 6 needles.

Abbreviations Beg-beginning; cm-centimetre(s); cont-continu(e)(ing); dec-decreas(e)(ing); foll-follow(s)(ing); g-gramme(s); in-inch(es); inc-increas(e)(ing); K-knit; mm-millimetre(s); No.-number; oz-ounce(s); P-purl; patt-pattern; rem-remain(s)(ing); rep-repeat(ing); st(s)-stitch(es); sl-slip.

BACK
** Using 3¼ mm/No. 4 needles, cast on 66(74:82:86) sts.
Cont in K1, P1 rib until work measures 5 cm/2 in from beg.
Next row Rib 4(8:12:5), [inc in next st, rib 2(2:2:3)] 19 times, inc in next st, rib to end. 86(94:102:106) sts.
Change to 4 mm/No. 6 needles and cont in patt.
1st row (right side) K1, * K2, P2, rep from * to last st, P1.
2nd row As 1st row.
3rd row P1, * P2, K2, rep from * to last st, K1.
4th row As 3rd row.
These 4 rows form the patt. ** Cont in patt until work measures 47(51:55:59) cm/18½(20:21¾:23¼) in from beg, ending with a wrong side row.
Shape Shoulders
Cast/bind off 28(31:34:35) sts at beg of next 2 rows.
Leave the rem 30(32:34:36) sts on a spare needle.

FRONT
Work as for Back from ** to **.
Cont in patt until work measures 30 rows less than Back to shoulder, ending with a wrong side row.
Shape Neck
Next row Patt 38(41:44:45) sts, turn and patt to end, leaving rem sts on a spare needle.
Cont on these sts only for left side of neck.
Dec one st at neck edge on next and every foll 3rd row until 28(31:34:25) sts rem, ending at armhole edge.
Shape Shoulder
Cast/bind off the rem sts.
With right side of work facing, return to sts on spare needle, sl centre 10(12:14:16) sts onto a holder, rejoin yarn at neck edge, patt to end.
Complete as for first side of neck.

SLEEVES
Using 3¼ mm/No. 4 needles, cast on 36(38:40:42) sts.

Cont in K1, P1 rib until work measures 5 cm/2 in from beg.
Next row Rib 4(8:6:5), [inc in next st, rib 2(1:1:1)] 9(11:13:15) times, inc in next st, rib to end. 46(50:54:56) sts.
Change to 4 mm/No. 6 needles and cont in patt as for Back, inc one st at each end of next and every foll 5th row until there are 82(86:96:100) sts.
Cont without shaping until work measures 30(32:34:36) cm/12(12½:13½:14¼) in from beg, ending with a wrong side row.
Cast/bind off **loosely**.

TO MAKE UP
Join shoulder seams.

COLLAR
Using 3¼ mm/No. 4 circular needle and with right side of work facing, beg at centre of sts on holder at front neck, K across first 5(6:7:8) sts, K up 28 sts up right side of neck, K across 30(32:34:36) sts at back neck, K up 28 sts down left side of neck and K across rem 5(6:7:8) at centre front. 96(100:104:108) sts.
Work in rounds of K1, P1 rib until collar measures 3 cm/1¼ in, ending at centre front neck.
Now commence working in rows.
Next row Rib 10, [inc in next st] 76(80:84:88) times, rib 10. 172(180:188:196) sts.
Cont in rib as set until collar measures 12 cm/4¾ in from beg.
Cast/bind off **loosely** in rib.
Set in sleeves, placing centre of cast/bound off edge to shoulder seams. Join side and sleeve seams.

SOURCE GUIDE

For local stockists in each country write to the manufacturers listed below:

GREAT BRITAIN

Argyll Wools Ltd., R. & D. Bishop, 3rd Avenue, Pioneer Market, Ilford, Essex, Great Britain

Emu, Leeds Road, Greengates, Bradford, West Yorkshire, BD10 9TE, Great Britain

Hayfield Textiles Ltd., Hayfield Mills, Glusburn, Nth Keighley, West Yorkshire, BD20 8QP, Great Britain

Lister/Lee, George Lee & Sons Ltd., Whiteoak Mills, Westgate, Wakefield, West Yorkshire, WF2 9SF, Great Britain

Patons, Patons and Baldwins Ltd., Alloa, Clackmannanshire, Scotland, Great Britain

Phildar, 4 Gamerel Road, Westgate Industrial Estate, Northampton, NN5 5NF, Great Britain

Pingouin, French Wools Ltd., 7–11 Lexington Street, London, W1R 4BU, Great Britain

Robin Wools Ltd., Robin Mills, Bradford, West Yorkshire, BD10 9TE, Great Britain

Rowan, Green Lane Mill, Washpit, Holmfirth, West Yorkshire, HD7 1RW, Great Britain

Schachenmayer, C/- Aero, Aero Group PLC., Box 2, Edward Street, Redditch, Worcs., B97 6HB, Great Britain

Scheepjeswol UK Ltd., 7 Colemeadow Road, North Moons Moat, Redditch, Worcs., B98 9NZ, Great Britain

Sirdar, Sirdar PLC., Flanshaw Lane, Alverthorpe, Wakefield, West Yorkshire, WF2 9ND, Great Britain

Sunbeam, Sunbeam Wools, Crawshaw Mills, Robin Lane, Pudsey, West Yorkshire, LS28 7BS, Great Britain

Twilleys, H. G. Twilley Ltd., Roman Mill, Stamford, Lincs., PE9 1BG, Great Britain

Wendy Wools, Carter and Parker Ltd., Gordon Mills, Netherfield Road, Guisely, West Yorkshire, LS20 9PD, Great Britain

AUSTRALIA

Hayfield Textiles Ltd., Panda Yarns (International) Ltd., 17–27 Brunswick Road, East Brunswick, Victoria 3057, Australia

Patons, Coats & Patons Australia Ltd., P.O. Box 110, Mount Waverley, Victoria 3149, Australia

Pingouin, C. Sullivan Pty Ltd., 3 Ralph Avenue, Alexandria, NSW 2015, Australia

Scheepjeswol, Thorobred Scheepjeswol, 762 High Street, East Kew, Victoria 3102, Australia

Sirdar, Sirdar (Australia) Pty Ltd., P.O. Box 110, Mt Waverley, Victoria 3149, Australia

Twilleys. See Panda Yarns listed under Hayfield Textiles Ltd.

Wendy Wool, Craft Warehouse, 30 Guess Avenue, Arncliffe, NSW 2205, Australia

CANADA

Argyll Wools Ltd., Estelle Designs & Sales Ltd., 1135 Queen Street East, Toronto, Canada

Hayfield Textiles Ltd., Craftsmen Distributors Inc., 4166 Halifax Street, Burnaby, British Columbia V56 3X2, Canada

Lister/Lee, Yarn Plus, 120/5726 Burleigh Crescent, Calgary, Alberta, Canada

Patons, Patons & Baldwins Ltd., 1001 Roselawn Avenue, Toronto, Ontario M6B 1B8, Canada

Phildar, Phildar Ltd., 6200 Est Boulevard H Bourassa, Montreal Nord H1G 5X3, Canada

Pingouin, 1500 Rue Jules Poitras, 379 St Laurent, Quebec H4N 1X7, Canada

Scheepjeswol, Scheepjeswol Ltd., 400 B Montee de Liese, Montreal, Quebec H4T 1NB, Canada

Sirdar, The Diamond Yarn Corp., 9697 St Laurence Boulevard, Montreal, Canada

Sunbeam, Estelle Designs & Sales Ltd., 1135 Queen Street East, Toronto, Ontario M4M 1K9, Canada

Wendy Wools, White Buffalo Mills Ltd., 6365 Kestrel Road, Mississauga, Ontario, Canada

NEW ZEALAND

Patons, Coats Patons Ltd., P.O. Box 50–140, Mohuia Crescent, Elsdon, Porirua, Wellington, New Zealand

Scheepjeswol, Thorobred Scheepjeswol Ltd., P.O. Box 52–028, 300 Richmond Road, Grey Lynn, Kingsland, Auckland 3, New Zealand

Sirdar, Alltex International, P.O. Box 2500, 106 Parnell Road, Auckland, New Zealand

Wendy Wools, Wendy Wool New Zealand Ltd., P.O. Box 29107, Greenwoods Corner, Auckland, New Zealand

UNITED STATES

Hayfield Textiles Ltd., Shepherd Wools Inc., 711 Johnson Avenue, Blaine, Washington 98230, USA

Patons, Susan Bates Inc., 212 Middlesex Avenue, Route 9A, Chester, Connecticut 06412, USA

Phildar, Phildar Inc., 6438 Dawson Boulevard, 85 North Norcross, Georgia 30093, USA

Pingouin, V. Hoover Promafil Corporation, P.O. Box 100, Jamestown, South Carolina, USA

Rowan, Westminster Trading, 5 Northern Boulevard, Amhurst, New Hampshire 03031, USA

Schachenmayer, Leisure Arts Inc., P.O. Box 5595, Little Rock, Arkansas 72215, USA

Scheepjeswol, Scheepjeswol USA Inc., 155 Lafayette Avenue, North White Plains, New York 10603, USA

Sirdar, Kendex Corporation, 31332 Via Colinas 107, Westlake Village, California 91362, USA

Sunbeam, Pirates Cove, Box 57, Babylon, New York 11702, USA